Georges Bizet

A Biography

Christoph Schwandt
Translated by Cynthia Klohr

THE SCARECROW PRESS, INC.
Lanham • Toronto • Plymouth, UK
2013

Published by Scarecrow Press, Inc.
A wholly owned subsidiary of The Rowman & Littlefield Publishing Group, Inc.
4501 Forbes Boulevard, Suite 200, Lanham, Maryland 20706
www.rowman.com

10 Thornbury Road, Plymouth PL6 7PP, United Kingdom

Title of the original German edition: *Georges Bizet: Eine Biografie*, written by Christoph Schwandt, Reinbeck, 1991
© 2011 SCHOTT MUSIC, Mainz, Germany
English language edition © 2013 by Cynthia Klohr

British Library Cataloguing in Publication Information Available

Library of Congress Cataloging-in-Publication Data

Schwandt, Christoph, 1956–
  [Georges Bizet. English]
  Georges Bizet : a biography / Christoph Schwandt ; translated by Cynthia Klohr.
      pages cm
  Translated from the German edition: Georges Bizet : Eine Biografie, 2011.
  Includes bibliographical references and index.
  ISBN 978-0-8108-8618-6 (cloth : alk. paper) — ISBN 978-0-8108-8619-3 (ebook)
  1. Bizet, Georges, 1838-1875. 2. Composers—France—Biography. I. Klohr, Cynthia, 1954-, translator. II. Title.
  ML410.B62S2813 2013
  780.92—dc23
  [B]
                                                              2012051708

∞™ The paper used in this publication meets the minimum requirements of American National Standard for Information Sciences—Permanence of Paper for Printed Library Materials, ANSI/NISO Z39.48-1992. Printed in the United States of America.

Contents

Chapter 1   Eclipsed by His Own Masterpiece   1

Chapter 2   The Boy at the Conservatory, 1848–1855   5

Chapter 3   Skill, Knowledge, and Ideas, 1855–1856   19

Chapter 4   Off to Rome for *Clovis and Clotilde*, 1856–1859   27

Chapter 5   Instead of a Mass, an Opera Buffa, 1859   37

Chapter 6   *Vasco da Gama* and *Roma*, 1859–1860   45

Chapter 7   Back in the Capital, 1861–1862   51

Chapter 8   Ivan the Terrible and *Leïla*, 1863–1865   59

Chapter 9   Arrangements and Rhine Romanticism, 1865–1866   69

Chapter 10   A Gypsy in Scotland, 1866–1868   77

Chapter 11   No New Opera, but Marriage and War, 1868–1871   89

Chapter 12   Masterpieces—*Jeux d'enfants* and *Djamileh*, 1871–1872   99

Chapter 13   Successful Music for a Failed Play, 1872–1873   107

Chapter 14   *Carmen*, an Opéra Comique   117

               Selected Bibliography   135

               Title Index   137

               Name Index   139

CHAPTER ONE

Eclipsed by His Own Masterpiece

Georges Bizet wrote the music for the opera *Carmen*. He became renowned solely for having done so, though not during his lifetime. He has come to be seen exclusively in light of that work. But making a "one-work composer" out of him for the sake of opera history—as German audiences erroneously also did to Charles Gounod (*Faust*), Ruggero Leoncavallo (*Pagliacci*), and Bedřich Smetana (*The Bartered Bride*)—obscures the fact that Bizet was an important musician of his own day. To make matters worse, *Carmen* did not become widespread in the form Bizet intended, but based on an edited version that omitted some of Bizet's passages and added others taken from alien sources. The glare focused on Bizet's *Carmen* leaves the rest of his oeuvre and life in the dark.

"I'm convinced that in ten years *Carmen* will be the most popular opera the world over. But prophets are ignored at home. *Carmen* was not really successful in Paris. Bizet died young in his best years shortly after it was shown. Of disappointment?" wrote Peter I. Tchaikovsky.[1] Tchaikovsky's own opera *Queen of Spades* evokes Bizet's musical dramaturgy and his ballet *Nutcracker* was clearly inspired by Bizet's style of instrumentation.

That Bizet died of a broken composer's heart was a widespread rumor lacking proof. His provocative opera bewildered conservative audiences, and being chronically ill, his untimely death spawned rumors that he had been a grievously melancholy musician. Late nineteenth-century music historians loved the cliché.

"Of modest means, he accepted menial jobs to earn a living."[2] Claims like this have been almost habitually woven into booklet texts for recordings of Bizet's music, especially *Carmen*, and added to visual material from stage productions. Unlike Giacomo Meyerbeer, Bizet's work never made him particularly wealthy, and he never enjoyed the material security enabled, let's say, by a professorship. But on the other hand, unlike Wagner, Bizet was never plagued by debt, and unlike many composers of his time, he was never in need of a second occupation just to feed his family. Bizet's financial circumstances were good; he was respected socially and was made a member of the Legion of Honor.

Carmen did by far become the most popular opera ever. Even individual stage works by Mozart, Verdi, and Puccini, not to mention Wagner, cannot compete with *Carmen* because they are all tied to a central-European notion of the theater in a way that *Carmen* is not. *Carmen* has been recorded several times in Russian, and even in Mandarin Chinese.[3] Bizet's opera *Carmen* made Prosper Mérimée's novella part of world literature. Mérimée's tale became inseparably associated with Bizet's congenial music and adapted for many purposes: it was used for ballet based on Bizet's original score and paraphrased by Rodion Shchedrin;[4] it was used for a silent movie (in 1918, starring Ernst Lubitsch and Pola Negri) with a background piano playing in Bizet style; it was used for a luxurious cinema version of the opera and made into the Hollywood musical *Carmen Jones* with songs by Oscar Hammerstein (directed by Otto Preminger); Peter Brook used *Carmen* for avant garde musical theater and Carlos Saura used it to combine dance and film.

Georges Bizet became one of the most frequently played composers, although except for *Carmen* and two suites that include parts from that opera (only one of which was authorized), the only other pieces by him that can be found on today's concert programs (most often concerts of so-called "popular classic") are orchestra suites from *L'Arlésienne*. And of those, the second one is not even by Bizet.

Oddly enough, Spain, the showplace of his extremely successful opera, made Parisian musician Bizet, whose only real trip abroad was to Italy,[5] famous for having immortalized *España* in allegedly authentic music. And yet, the music in *Carmen* is no more and no less Spanish than Mozart's music for *Figaro* or Beethoven's music for *Fidelio*, both of which also take place in Seville.

In 1949, Walter Klefisch, the first German translator and editor of Bizet's correspondence, noted correctly that "the history of Bizet's life is for the most part identical with the history of his works."[6] But today even that approach to appreciating Bizet won't do. There exists no complete critical edition of his works. The only broad scientific study of Bizet's compositions prior to *Carmen* revealed "a century of textual corruption."[7]

Bizet's first symphony is an ingenious early work that was not rediscovered until fifty years after his death. Until then it was considered insignificant, even by those who safely archived it. No one took inventory of the musician's remaining papers; no one bundled them for posterity. Bizet's heirs carelessly discarded relevant correspondence, and many other documents were lost in the Second World War, having never undergone any critical evaluation. Eleven years after Bizet's death, Charles Pigot, Bizet's first biographer, reported as facts things and events that he can only have heard from third parties, undertaking—as was common for the times—nothing to verify them. By what we know today, much of what he related is improbable.

For the German-speaking public it became difficult to discuss Georges Bizet and his work with insight and fairness once Friedrich Nietzsche had dragged Bizet's name into a heated dispute over Wagner. Even more aggravating is that the philosopher's anti-Wagnerian eulogy for Bizet and *Carmen* appears to have been written on a whim.[8] Nietzsche's remarks on Bizet's opera were based on questionable performances sung in Italian that he had attended in Genoa and Turin; his remarks he noted in the margin[9] of a German version of *Carmen* translated by Julius Hopp; in other words, Nietzsche was going by distorted versions of Bizet's aesthetics and dramaturgy to begin with.

Music specialists did the rest by for the most part neglecting Bizet—except for *Carmen*. Only two books on Bizet were written in German. One was a well-founded overview of Bizet's life and work written by Paul Stefan Grünfeld, who died in American exile in 1943 while completing it. The other, by Adolf Weissmann, was published in Berlin in 1907. Weissmann wrote that Bizet "was most richly blessed with the tragic privilege awarded the great, namely, to be misunderstood. Why? We have no idea. Germans had a right to misunderstand Wagner; but only the French could misunderstand Bizet. And as a matter of fact, Bizet was almost the only one who understood Wagner well enough to shun him. *Carmen* had just barely been introduced to German audiences, when one felt called to teach the French how to honor their own prophet."[10] Even respected musicologist Guido Adler perpetuated misconceptions and rumors, such as the alleged existence of three other symphonies written by Bizet (besides the orchestra suites), even suggesting that "Bizet began with operettas."[11] Even critic Eduard Hanslick, who probably was not familiar with the works themselves, called *Les Pêcheurs de perles* and *La Jolie fille de Perth* "comic operas" and claimed that the composer had been an amazing, award-winning wunderkind.[12]

By the early twenty-first century, other works by Bizet have now finally gotten more of the notice they deserve, but most of the false beliefs about the composer live on.

Notes

1. Letter to Nadezhda von Meck dated 18 (30) July 1880, found in *Teure Freundin: Peter Tschaikowskys Briefwechsel mit Nadeshda von Meck*, trans. by Ena von Baer (Leipzig, 1964).

2. Erika Krökel, 1975, in a text accompanying the record Eterna 826623, a recording of music for the orchestra by Bizet.

3. Featuring Qing Miao in the title role; recording of a performance in Beijing in 1982, directed by French conductor Jean Périsson.

4. Shchedrin's *Carmen Suite* also contains other work by Bizet that in turn was later used for ballet segments in *Carmen* opera performances. The Russian composer was not familiar with Bizet's original opera score for *Carmen*.

5. Bizet took two short trips—one to Brussels and the other to the grand duchy of Baden, neither of which took him far from French influence.

6. Walter Klefisch, ed., *Georges Bizet: Briefe aus Rom* (Hamburg, 1949), 6.

7. Leslie Allison Wright, *Bizet before Carmen* (Ann Arbor, Mich., 1983), 10.

8. In a letter to Carl Fuchs dated 27 December 1888, Nietzsche wrote: "Don't take what I say about Bizet all too seriously; the way I am, Bizet is just not my kind of composer. But using him as an ironic antithesis to Wagner makes a strong case." Taken from *Werke* [Works], ed. Karl Schlechta (Munich, 1956), 3:1347.

9. See Hugo Daffner, *Nietzsches Randglossen zu Bizets Carmen* [Nietzsche's marginalia on Bizet's *Carmen*] (Regensburg, appeared undated in 1921).

10. Adolf Weissmann, *Bizet* (Berlin, 1907), 3.

11. Guido Adler, *Handbuch der Musikgeschichte* [Handbook on the history of music] (Berlin, 1930), 899.

12. Eduard Hanslick, *Aus neuer und neuester Zeit* [From modern and most modern times] (Berlin 1900), 121f.

CHAPTER TWO

The Boy at the
Conservatory, 1848–1855

Georges Bizet was born to parents that set him on the path to music. They were much more than simply a "musical family" of the educated bourgeoisie. The Bizet family's efforts in music had taken them from being common artisans to become respected members of the middle class. Georges's father Adolphe Bizet (1810–1886) had been born in Rouen. Having just moved to Paris, in 1837 he married Aimée Delsarte, who was five years younger. Marriage documents state that he was a hairdresser and wig maker. But by the time son Alexandre César Léopold—nicknamed Georges—was born, Adolphe Bizet had become a teacher for singing.

All of his life, Adolphe Bizet had had an urge to be involved in music; wig making probably followed from an insight that his musical talent was less than outstanding. Nonetheless, he did compose a bit of music that can still be found in archives—although it admittedly deserves only anecdotal mention. He was more successful at teaching song: Hector Gruyer, one of his pupils, was considered for the title role in the premiere production of Charles Gounod's *Faust*, but was unable to meet the unusual demands made by the part. After changing his name to Guardi, Gruyer did go on to have a successful career in Italy, however, and back home in France he was made a member of the Legion of Honor.

Georges Bizet's mother, too, was from northern France, born in Cambrai to a family that not only had a profound interest in art, but also other interests that were fairly unconventional considering their bourgeois circumstances. Aimée's father, Jean-Nicolas Delsarte (there exists no proof that the name had any Italian or Spanish origin) brought his family almost to the brink of ruin by becoming an inventor, after equally unsuccessfully trying his hand at law, running a café, and trading in wine. In Paris one of his sons, François Alexandre Delsarte, became a respected teacher of song and known as the editor of works by Lully, Gluck, and Rameau published in *Les Archives du chant*. François later began teaching acting and body movement on the stage. After his death one of his pupils dubbed his work the "Delsarte Method" and made it popular in the United States; it considerably influenced modern dance of the early twentieth century.

The home of the Bizets in Paris's rue de la Tour d'Auvergne, no. 26 (the family later moved a few houses farther down the same street) was filled with music. Their son, born on 25 October 1838, listened to his father at the piano and heard his father's pupils singing. His mother, to whom Georges

François Delsarte

Bizet's place of birth (second house from the left) on rue de la Tour d'Auvergne. *Courtesy of C. Schwandt*

was very attached, is also said to have played the piano well; Aimée taught Georges not only to read, but to read music as well. Bizet's first break in life as a musician was simultaneously the first time he was separated from his mother: at the age of nineteen he left his hometown Paris to travel to Italy via Provence. Georges was a thoroughly Parisian boy and by no means of a Mediterranean nature—especially not of the Spanish kind that due to *Carmen* posterity has come to think that he embodied.

Naturally, young Georges learned to play the piano. In the mid-nineteenth century the piano was not just an instrument to play, it had a purpose later fulfilled by electronic media, recordings, and playback equipment: it enabled one to become familiar with symphonies and operas by playing their scores and piano arrangements. We can assume that at the home of song teacher Adolphe Bizet one heard not only Mozart and Beethoven classics, that is, not only their works for the piano, but also two- and four-handed arrangements of their symphonies, along with piano arrangements for operas by Auber, Boieldieu, Bellini, and Donizetti that were popular at the time. Singing lessons will also have involved songs by fashionable French composers and the indispensable Old Italian masters.

At the piano Bizet developed his musical imagination that later grew to the sense of tone color and the transparency in orchestral movements so characteristic of his mature compositions. He surely also read books that were typical for the times. We have no proof, as has been sometimes said, that he was wholly ignorant of literature, just as there is no evidence that he had any exceptional literary preferences while growing up. Although schooling was not compulsory, we can assume that he enjoyed the general education common for a child of his background. At the home of his uncle François Delsarte, Georges joined the singing lessons that his aunt Rosine gave to his cousins. Rosine was the daughter of a well-known opera singer. Mentored by Luigi Cherubini, at the age of just thirteen she had become an assistant teacher at the Paris Conservatory.

Bizet's parents recognized their son's intuition for music and his talent at the piano. He could easily sing or play pieces he had heard just once. It was soon decided that the boy needed professional training.

Georges, however, had not yet turned ten, the minimum age for acceptance to the Paris Conservatory under the direction of Daniel-François-Esprit Auber. A friend of Bizet's father arranged a meeting with Joseph Émile Meifred, a horn player and member of the student advisory committee at the conservatory, in an attempt to get his son accepted anyway. Classes had no vacancies, but Uncle Delsarte's connections enabled Georges to unofficially enjoy instruction at the piano by Antoine François Marmontel. In October 1848—he had still not yet turned ten—Georges Bizet was registered at the conservatory as a regular pupil. After just one year of solfège, the technique used for training one's ear and for basic training in singing, Bizet won the first prize in the conservatory's competition. (Today the French system of education, geared to elitism and tradition, still founds evaluation on this custom of competing for prizes through regular examinations.)

In 1849 an American child prodigy joined Marmontel's piano class: twelve-year-old Ernest Guiraud. Bizet quickly made friends with the boy just one year older than himself, the son of a French musician that had immigrated to America. In 1827 Ernest's father, Jean-Baptiste Guiraud, had won

Antoine François Marmontel, Bizet's first piano teacher. *Bibliothèque Nationale, Paris*

the first prize in a composition competition for the *Prix de Rome*, the same year that Hector Berlioz participated for the first time, and unsuccessfully, in the same competition. Having won the prize, Jean-Baptiste Guiraud was permitted to write an opera (*Charles V et Duguesclin*) together with his peer Alphonse Gilbert for production in Paris in 1827. The piece was a failure. But Jean-Baptiste's son Ernest was just as ambitious as his father. He wrote the opera *David* that was eventually performed on stage in 1853 in his native city, New Orleans.

Georges Bizet's curriculum at the conservatory was soon augmented by private instruction in composition and counterpoint from elderly Pierre Joseph Guillaume Zimmermann, who was instantly thrilled by his new pupil's talent. Zimmermann had studied under Luigi Cherubini, and one of his own students (later to become his son-in-law) was Charles Gounod, who occasionally substituted for him in giving Bizet his lessons. After long preparation among the Carmelites, Gounod had decided against becoming a priest. Thus even as a boy Georges Bizet knew important contemporary Parisian opera composers and was familiar with their tradition. Charles Gounod, twenty years Georges's senior, mentored him throughout his short life, offering fatherly and collegial friendship and encouragement.

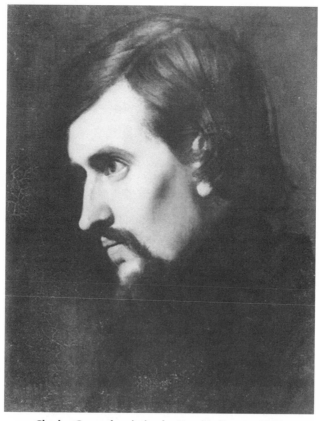

Charles Gounod, painting by Henri Lehmann, 1841

The year that Georges Bizet was born, 1838, was the eighth year of rule by the so-called *roi citoyen* (citizen king), under whom being a citizen primarily meant being a member of the upper class. In the February revolution of 1848, republicans overthrew Louis-Philippe. The following December, Napoleon I's nephew Prince Louis-Napoléon was elected president; in 1852 he declared himself Emperor Napoleon III.

Outwardly, Paris was still very much a city shaped by prerevolutionary times, but it began to increasingly attract people from the provinces and from abroad. Napoleon III and Georges-Eugène Haussmann, his prefect from the *département* Seine, soon went about creating an entirely new cityscape by making generous and radical changes. Paris continued to grow and by 1860 had 1.7 million inhabitants (Berlin had less than a third of that number at the time). In other words, the city that young Georges Bizet knew day in and day out was marked by gigantic urban renewal work: old streets and quarters were being torn down to make room for spacious new boulevards, avenues, and roads that today still shape the face of Paris. These changes to the old community—some of which were quite brutal—were not simply matters of hygiene (particularly sewage control) and traffic: Paris's new look was a prestigious matter for the *Grande Nation*. Urban lifestyle was considered the epitome of civilization. There was no greater contrast to life in the country than the impression one got when coming from Provence to Paris during those years. Napoleon III wanted to have the most beautiful and most modern capital that would also be a metropolitan cultural center. Among other things, Haussmann planned the Palais Garnier, the new building for the Grand Opéra. The first opera stage in Paris, the Théâtre de l'Académie Royale de Musique founded by Louis XIV, played on rue Lepeletier; the Opéra Comique, which had also already existed for over a century, stood on rue Favart.

"Opéra comique" meant a kind of musical stage production that included spoken dialogue. Originally the stories shown at the Opéra Comique were, in fact, purely humorous. The "music numbers" performed there were songs complete in themselves and more accessible than arias and choir pieces performed at the Grand Opéra where the music was, indeed, more consistent, but where visual effects were often more important than plot dynamics. Grand opera presented an artistic and approved expression of the period of Bourbon Restoration's own view of itself, just as later Jacques Offenbach's works would critically reflect the Second Empire. The latter evolved from carefree elements of opéra comique. But meanwhile the Opéra Comique itself had begun showing serious works and earnest characters alongside the bufforesque shows.

While Bizet attended the conservatory and his taste for opera was grow-ing, Paris's stages were successfully producing Boieldieu's *La Dame blanche* and Auber's *The Deaf Girl of Portici,* works by Hérold, Méhul, Jacques Fromental Halévy, and Adolphe Adam, as well as operettas by Florimond Hervé, and soon also by Offenbach. In 1838, the year that Georges Bizet was born, Hector Berlioz had completed his opera *Benvenuto Cellini,* after eight years previously having written his groundbreaking *Fantastic Symphony.* In 1836 Meyerbeer's *Huguenots* had premiered in Paris. Besides French com-posers, the opera houses also staged works by Luigi Cherubini and Gaspare Spontini that can be counted as belonging to French opera tradition. But Paris also engaged separate Italian opera companies and staged operas by Vincenzo Bellini, Gaetano Donizetti, Gioachino Rossini, and other now less well-known Italian composers. In an effort to accommodate Parisian taste, Donizetti and Rossini had also written operas in French for performance there.[1] In 1847 even young Giuseppe Verdi rewrote *Lombardi* to be staged as the not entirely new French opera *Jérusalem* at the house on rue Lepeletier. In Germany Weber, Marschner, Lortzing, Flotow, young Wagner, and Mey-erbeer were popular.

The few reports that exist recount little of what young Bizet might have thought of the opera he saw on Parisian stages. Most of the composers were influential members of the capital's musical scene, whom it would have been favorable to know well.

Bizet's first known compositions as a pupil of the conservatory are dated as having been written in the spring of 1850. These were so-called French *vocalises,* in other words, exercises in solfège, perhaps written for his father's pupils. During his early years at the conservatory Bizet also wrote short pieces for the piano. We know that in 1851 he attended the premiere for Gounod's new opera *Sappho.*

But for all of his growing interest in the theater, Bizet's study concentrated on working with Marmontel. The piano allowed him to express himself and to discover the music of others. By virtuoso standards he was not a wun-derkind at the piano, for despite his extreme talent in 1851 he did not win the *premier prix* at his first attempt to do so—presenting, after all, Chopin's concert in F minor. At his second try he won the prize—but shared it with another pupil.

After just four years of study under Marmontel, learning the mandatory pianistic repertoire—Bach, Mozart, Beethoven, Handel, and works by the French *clavecinists*—in 1852 Georges Bizet entered François Benoist's class for the organ. Georges's upbringing was by no means particularly religious. Adolphe Bizet had belonged to the anti-Roman Église Catholique Française.

The Paris Conservatoire

But his son discovered the organ surely for purely musical reasons and not, as many others did, in an effort to unite musicality with belief. It was important for the young musician to learn fugue skills, and that could be done under Benoist. The latter had been the *chef de chant* at the Opéra, responsible for its soloists learning their parts. Benoist had also tried his hand at writing worldly music: together with Ambroise Thomas and others, in 1839 and at the request of the Opéra he had written music for the ballet *La Gipsy*, starring the brilliant ballerina Fanny Elssler, who five years later married Louis-Désiré Véron, the Opéra's director.

Although his affinity to vocal music was becoming ever clearer, Bizet was not drawn to church music. Even pious Charles Gounod could not change that. The fact that posterity put liturgical texts to Bizet's melodies would probably have amused him.

Pierre Zimmermann died in 1853, and Jacques François Fromental Élie Halévy became Bizet's new teacher for composition. The latter's father had still gone by the name of Lévy and had come to France from the German

Jacques Fromental Halévy

city of Fürth. When Bizet joined his class, Halévy, born in 1799 in Paris, had already taught at the conservatory for twenty years, having studied there himself, and like Bizet, he had entered the conservatory before turning ten. Like Zimmermann, Halévy had studied under Cherubini, and had also been *chef de chant* for the Opéra from 1833 until 1845. He wrote several exuberant operas styled after Auber and Boieldieu. But his greatest and most lasting success was *La Juive* that premiered in 1835. It is a grand opera that follows Meyerbeer's model; in other words, it is voluminous, dramatic, elaborate, and five acts long. Richard Wagner found Halévy's talent "solemn and highly tragic," saying that he "entirely banished what is common or trivial, keeping every facet in line with the whole," and that his music had "dramatic melody."[2]

But when Bizet became Halévy's pupil, grand opera had long passed its creative zenith. In his own way, Meyerbeer had abandoned the rigid form of number music and developed a dramatic effect in opera. But in the end his creative musical talent was not on par with his trustworthy instinct for the stage. He had skillfully reflected the *zeitgeist* between two revolutions, accommodated the taste of the growing urban citizenry, and satisfied the demand for representative coups de théâtre.

In 1847, after having seen the premiering of young Giuseppe Verdi's opera *I due Foscari*, Heinrich Heine, who lived in Paris as of 1831, wrote: "I don't know whether it's a masterpiece, but it's fresh and original. In the absence of good work the audience is content with novelty. Verdi is the man of the day in the world of music now that Bellini is dead, Rossini and Donizetti are living dead, and Meyerbeer, too, has that fatal look on his face. He is as good as dead with the audiences here. As much as we would like to deny it, in the end we have to admit that the artificial and expensive machinery of Meyerbeer's fame has stalled. Did the delicate gears lose a screw?"[3]

Opéra comique, too, had outlived the once highly respected genre; the time was ripe for Jacques Offenbach and his new, entertaining kind of musical theater. When he began instruction under an esteemed opera composer, fifteen-year-old Bizet may have sensed that the days of conventional opera were a thing of the past. Ernest Guiraud, too, switched over to Halévy's class. Although it had originally been his explicit intention, Bizet's peer did not become a noteworthy opera composer, but he did become a teacher at the conservatory, later instructing Claude Debussy, Erik Satie, and Paul Dukas.

Before becoming Halévy's pupil, Bizet had written a few pieces for the piano that were later found among his remaining papers in a folder marked *diverse compositions*. He would have written these between the age of thirteen and fifteen. Four aphoristic preludes tell us much about the teenager's musical imagination. The first begins very unpianistic like a piano arrangement for an opera overture with a fanfare-like opening motif. Here he obviously took Chopin as a model for the left hand, and his polyphone phrases follow Bach. The emotional closing passages suggest that it was not intended as piano music in the narrower sense, but was a sketch for an orchestra work. Although Bizet had carefully studied classical and preclassical models, unlike many significant composers who produced early works that reveal nothing other than, for instance, an attempt to create a real sonata, nowhere does Bizet indicate any ambition to simply emulate traditional forms.

Bizet's first *Valse en ut majeur* with its characteristic repetitive and suspended notes and an agogic achieved by melody formation and accompanying figures is once again reminiscent of Chopin. Another of his very early surviving works, a short piece titled *Theme*, has such a broad style, pianistic emphasis, and efficient simplicity in the leading motif that it may have been a theme for later variation, but never got past being a theme. Except for one striking case, Bizet never spent time working out variations, although that was a common exercise for budding composers. But he did write *romances sans paroles*, the fashionable songs without words.

In September 1854, at the age of fifteen, Bizet marked one of his works, the *Grande valse de concert*, as Opus no. 1. It was less original than some of his earlier pieces, but it was at least formally developed in full and comparable to what at the time was popular for that conventional genre. Another piece for the piano, the *Premiere nocturne en fa majeur*, about seven minutes in length, is also dated from 1854 and exhibits much more creative individualism.

At about this time, Bizet began combining words with music.[4] Two of his short songs, "*Petite Marguerite*" and "*La Rose et l'abeille*" (Little Margaret and The Rose and the Bee), were published shortly after he turned sixteen. They were published together with songs written by his father in the *Magasin de musique du Conservatoire* edited by Mme. Cendrier.

His father's good connections also enabled Bizet to soon thereafter publish three short pieces for the piano in a series called *Albums de musique*, an extra for subscribers of the monthly *Magasin des familles*, an illustrated French family journal. The titles and degree of difficulty of these pieces indicate that they were intended for music making at home and designed to serve the taste of the general public. It attests to the young musician's sense of business, which was no less professional than the aesthetic side of his work. One is a *Song without Words*, another is called *Casilda*, referring most probably to a poem called *Saint Casilde* by Théophile Gautier[5] that describes the saint from a picture at a church in Burgos. The third piece is called *Méditation religieuse* and can be played on the organ or the harmonium.

Besides his own piano pieces, for the purpose of study as well as income Bizet wrote many arrangements for the works of other composers. Charles Gounod commissioned him to produce a piano arrangement for his opera *La Nonne sanglante* (The Bloodthirsty Nun) that he had rather unsuccessfully presented in October 1854. The text was by Eugène Scribe,[6] who, having written innumerous opera texts (thirty-eight for Auber alone), still guaranteed a libretto that would really work onstage. During this work, Bizet met publisher Antoine de Choudens.

In June 1855 the Opéra premiered Giuseppe Verdi's *Les Vêpres siciliennes* based on a text by Scribe and Charles Duvevrier. It was a French opera that had been ordered from the meanwhile famous Italian composer of *Rigoletto*, *La traviata*, and *Il trovatore* for quite a bit of money. That same year, Gounod published his first symphony in D minor. He asked Bizet to produce a piano arrangement for it. Once again the young musician demonstrated his reliable instinct at converting ideas created for an orchestra into the two notation systems used for the piano.

During Bizet's almost four years of study under Halévy (who was also the standing secretary for the Académie des Beaux-Arts), the latter composed two more works in comique style (*Jaguarita l'indienne* and the one-act piece *L'Inconsolable*) and also his grand opera *La Magicienne*, and began working on *Noé*, which his pupil would one day complete for him. We do not know what Bizet thought of Halévy's oeuvre. He was probably too diplomatic to jeopardize his career by criticizing his teacher, but also too upright and self-confident to pretend to highly acknowledge him. The fact that Georges later joined Halévy's family through marriage makes it very difficult to evaluate the relationship between the teacher and pupil objectively. Bizet's work did at least continue Halévy's style of "dramatic melody."

Halévy's wife, Hannah Léonie, was twenty-one years younger than her husband and came from a wealthy and cultivated Jewish family from Bordeaux. She was an intelligent, well-educated woman, a sculptress and art collector who entertained distinguished guests, including painter Eugène Delacroix. Her husband, naturally, also brought well-known musicians to their home. But Mme. Halévy also often stayed at Dr. Blanche's exclusive clinic on Montmartre for medical treatment of mental disorders. The Halévys had two daughters: Esther, born in 1843, and Geneviève, born six years later.

It was at the Halévy home that Georges Bizet also met the composer's nephew Ludovic Halévy, his senior by four years. Ludovic's father was Halévy's brother Leon (1802–1883), an archeologist by profession who also liked to write and had cooperated on the libretto for Jacques Fromental's early opera *La Dilettante d'Avignon*.

Notes

1. *The Daughter of the Regiment* and *The Favorite* (Donizetti, 1840) and *Le Comte Ory* and *William Tell* (Rossini, 1828 and 1829, respectively).

2. Richard Wagner, *Gesammelte Schriften*, ed. Julius Kapp (Leipzig, n.d.), 8:72f.

3. Musical column from Paris written for the newspaper *Allgemeine Zeitung*, dated 1 February 1847. In Heinrich Heine, *Über die französische Bühne*, ed. Christoph Trilse (Berlin, 1971), 494.

4. Winton Dean dates *L'Ame triste est pareille au doux ciel*, a song found among Bizet's remaining papers and based on a text by Alphonse de Lamartine, as definitely originating sometime "very early." See Winton Dean, *Bizet* (London, 1975), 266.

5. Bizet may have been familiar with Ernst II of Saxe-Coburg-Gotha's opera *Casilda* from 1851.

6. This libretto, as well as Scribe's text for Meyerbeer's *Robert le diable*, was based on Matthew Gregory Lewis's novel *The Monk*.

CHAPTER THREE

Skill, Knowledge, and Ideas, 1855–1856

Inspired by London's Great Exhibition of 1851, in 1855 Paris hosted a universal exposition for international commerce and industry intended to top the first, thereby establishing what came to be the tradition of world "expos." One of the accompanying expo festivities in late April that Bizet attended was the first performance of Hector Berlioz's monumental *Te Deum* at the church Saint-Eustache. Around that time Bizet was presumably trying to write a piece for the orchestra, an overture in A minor. In 1972 Antonio de Almeida published the score that had wandered—never performed—directly from Bizet's remaining papers to France's national library. It had been played for the first time in 1938 in Paris in celebration of the centenary of Bizet's birth.

Halévy never knew that in November 1855 his pupil had written an entire symphony. Except for a funeral march called *Le Cendres de Napoléon* (Napoleon's Ashes), written in 1840 on the occasion of the final interment of Napoleon Bonaparte's remains, Bizet's venerable teacher had never himself composed anything for the orchestra.

Working on the piano arrangement for Gounod's symphony was probably the moment when all the symphonic music that Bizet had heard and studied and absorbed with his keen musical mind, everything he had combined and further developed, began to solidify: he wanted to put his own ideas to the test of the great traditional form of the symphony. While in Gounod's first symphony we still hear Beethoven's Symphony no. 7 used as a model for the first two movements and that the third movement contains a typical Haydn/Mozart minuet, Bizet's first symphony emulated no one. The notion that Bizet never published his first symphony for fear of the accusation that he might have plagiarized Gounod's can be eliminated by simply comparing them.

The first three movements of Georges Bizet's Symphony in C Major follow the classical pattern of juxtaposing two antagonistic musical ideas. The work begins with a modest arpeggio introduced with verve in unison, contrasted with a softly settling cantilena. The second movement, the *Adagio*, begins with reserve but then immanently escalates, taking the listener far from the initially calm beginning and creating a clearly postclassical sound. It centers at first on an oboe melody,

a premonition of the mood of many an exotic, melancholy cantilena to turn up in Bizet's subsequent opera scores. A little fugato also testifies to the young composer's desire to shape things his way. He may have written this symphony just for practice, but it is a highly inspired, complete work. Its third movement is simply titled *Allegro* and follows the pattern of typical scherzos from greater models. It, too, has two antagonist strands and begins with the orchestra in lively unison followed by a songlike reply. Bizet easily plays these two principles against one another. The ironic tone of a trio-like segment with its robust drone fifths reveals a thoroughly self-confident stance toward traditional ways, once again underscored by a humorously diatonic treatment of the oboes.

In the fourth movement a light motoric motif prepares us for an optimistic wind instrument theme. The symphony then closes with an almost Beethoven-like, insistent

twist. But as if Bizet did not himself believe in Beethoven's pathos of the grand finale, he interrupts it briefly with a nonchalant wink from the flute.

Georges Bizet's symphony sounds light and unpretentious, but in many respects it is a composition of weight and significance: the musical ease is not trivial. Here the young composer proves that he can invent melodies, that his instinct for rhythm is reliable, and that he understands the art of instrumentation. In 1933 musicologist Jean Chantavoine drew attention to the manuscript found in the national library, but no one was interested. In 1935 British music historian Douglas Charles Parker, who in 1926 had written a Bizet biography, encouraged conductor Felix von Weingartner to premiere the eighty-year-old symphony by the meanwhile famous composer of *Carmen* in Basel, Switzerland.

After that initial premiering, no one in Germany took further note of Bizet's symphony. In 1943 Herbert Gerigk wrote in the foreword to the second edition of the *Lexikon der Juden in der Musik* (Lexicon of Jews in Music) that while Bizet had been married to the daughter of a Jewish teacher, he himself was Aryan, but "the Jews had claimed him a member of their race."[1] Regarding the very slow reception of Bizet's symphony, Egon Voss noted a "German tendency to think that pleasant and elegant music has to be superficial."[2]

Branded an "early work," Bizet's symphony was not taken into repertoires. But it is worth noting that at the age of seventeen Ludwig van Beethoven had not yet written even the very first of his "works without opus numbers," namely, *Musik zu einem Ritterballet,* which is widely acknowledged as being less significant, and Bizet's symphony can even bear comparison to Mozart's so-called little Symphony in G Minor (KV 183) written at the age of seventeen.

Like Sergei S. Prokofiev's cognate, brilliant *Classical Symphony* (Symphony no. 1 in D Major, op. 25), today Bizet's symphony is considered more "symphonic entertainment" than a piece of erudite work. The greater public is more familiar with it from numerous versions produced for ballet, foremost *Symphony in C* by George Balanchine. The work's four movements seem destined for elegant gesture and dance.

If we take Bizet's note on the original score seriously, the symphony was written very quickly and just after his seventeenth birthday.[3] At the same time he planned more seriously to write something for the stage. The short opéra comique *La Maison du docteur* (The Doctor's House) with its four fully composed song parts, for which only the piano arrangement without instrumentation has survived, shows that besides mastering the orchestra for a symphony, Bizet was also skilled at forming dramatically focused vocal characters: The daughter of a physician living near London, also known as a poison concocter, is secretly in love with two young men. Young Toby unexpectedly appears at their house seeking poison to commit suicide because an attempt with guns or rope might fail. The doctor's daughter discovers that Toby is both of the men she loves. Another patient, the bizarre and bored

Lord Harley, gives Toby money to pay the physician for the hand of his daughter. In return, Toby naively advises the elderly lord to marry, too, and suddenly the two find themselves rivals for the same woman. But instead of a duel there is a happy ending; the young couple promises to take Lord Harley into their family. . . .

The burlesque with its skilled couplets and short opera-like ensembles was probably performed by friends at home; at the time Georges Bizet would not have expected anything more because Gounod's friend Paul d'Ivry had already written music for the libretto and that version had been performed in Dijon in 1855. Bizet's *La Maison du docteur* was just a bit of practice. In the late twentieth century William Girard took Bizet's score for the piano arrangement and wrote a stylistically apposite version for the orchestra. It was performed for the first time in Austin, Texas, in 1989 and in English. In 2002 it was sung for the first time in French in Nogent-sur-Marne near Paris accompanied by a sole violin, clarinet, piano, and contrabass.

Halévy also familiarized his pupil with practical aspects of theater operations, recommending him to the director of the Opéra Comique to give him experience perhaps at helping opera singers learn their parts, accompanying them at the piano, writing arrangements, or even composing. He also encouraged Bizet to compete for the Prix de Rome.

In France the arts and humanities were shaped not only by having a central cultural capital that other European countries still striving to define themselves as nations did not have, they were also shaped by a national institution that had the last word on the established arts. The arts themselves were organized in a system of training that like the entire nation was centralized and elitist. At the head was the *Institut de France* that consisted of five academies. The oldest of them, the *Académie français*, had been founded in 1635, The *Académie des Beaux-Arts* was added in 1816 and included music. Young artists strove for recognition awarded according to a rigid system. Initially only artists in the visual and plastic arts were awarded the Prix de Rome. It was a five-year stipend for study that began with two years at the Villa Medici in Rome, where in 1666 Jean-Baptiste Colbert, a statesman under Louis XIV, had set up an *Académie de France*. The stay in Rome could be followed by time in Germany. Later composers were allowed to compete for the prize (that was awarded until the year 1968), but only students from the conservatory that had not reached the age of thirty. Hector Berlioz (1830) and Charles Gounod (1839) were awarded the Prix de Rome.

The crucial examination task for an aspirant to the Prix de Rome was to write a cantata for one or more solo voices and orchestra; the text was

La Maison du docteur, a page from the autograph of the piano score

given, and usually of a religious, ancient history, or chivalrous nature. In anticipation of the test Bizet seems to have tried his hand at that genre several times; many such sketches can be found among his remaining papers.[4] Compulsory exercises also included choral works for four voices. A piano arrangement written for one such exercise, titled *Valse avec chœur* and dated as originating in 1855, has survived. The young composer did not care much for the trivial, waltz-evoking text and in the end let everyone just sing "tra-la-la."

Cantatas had always played an important role in French music. The first of significance had been written by Marc-Antoine Charpentier and Rameau during the baroque period. The cantata form experienced a renaissance in the late eighteenth century because it allowed the expression of revolutionary pathos without necessitating a huge opera production. (In contrast to German religious cantatas, in France they did not always involve a choir.) But by around 1850 the cantata had come to be seen as a fairly dusty relic, tended mostly for the sole purpose of the Prix de Rome.

In 1856 the competition task was to write music for a cantata text on *David* penned by Mademoiselle de Montréal, who used a masculine pseudonym to conceal her true identity. It is not difficult to imagine that Bizet was not particularly fascinated by the conventional, fussy exercise. But the consolation prize that he did win for second place was at least a set of free tickets for Paris's stages.

That year, Paris celebrated the end of the Crimean War, sealed by a peace agreement with Russia, which had fought with England against France. Gustave Flaubert completed *Madame Bovary*. Parisian society took more interest in what went on at the Salle Choiseul. There, after having taking its first steps at a small improvised theater on the Champs-Élysées, Jacques Offenbach's *Bouffes-Parisiens*, a troupe for musical entertainment, had established itself. Offenbach realized that traditional opéra comique had seen its last days, and paved the way for the innovation of humorous musical theater.

As early as 1844 Offenbach had had public success by persiflaging Félicien David's *Le Désert* (The Desert), caricaturing the mounting Parisian mania for everything oriental. He began to seek pieces for a repertoire for this new kind of keen yet bantering musical theater. Eighteen-year-old Bizet was among those who followed Offenbach's call for works:

> The Theater of Bouffes-Parisiens will strive to recreate a simple and jovial genre. . . . Each piece should last about forty-five minutes, involve only three actors, and require an orchestra of at the most thirty musicians. To write one takes imagination and ability for full-fledged melodies. . . . In an attempt to discover adequate writers for the French stage I invite our young composers to participate in a little contest. The theater that I put at your disposal asks of you only three things: that you have skill, knowledge, and ideas.[5]

The text for which the young composers were asked to write music already existed: it was *Le Docteur miracle*, written by Léon Battu and Halévy's nephew Ludovic, and was (deviating from Offenbach's own specifications) written for four actors. The public was already familiar with one "Doctor Miracle" from the play *Les Contes d'Hoffmann* by Jules Barbier and Michel Carré, who incidentally did not borrow the name from E. T. A. Hoffmann. The jury for Offenbach's enterprise consisted of Halévy, Auber, Gounod, Scribe, and Ambroise Thomas.

The burlesque plot of *Le Docteur miracle* uses traditional schemes and characters: A young officer is in love with the daughter of a podesta (a mayor and judge of an Italian town) who does not particularly care for soldiers and who by no means desires one for a son-in-law. But the couple gets the better of him by having the officer enter the podesta's household as a servant under a false name, where he eventually prepares an omelet for the older man. Soon a message arrives, saying that "vengeance is sweet" and the omelet had been poisoned. A physician is summoned, and the swaggering, Latin-spouting miracle doctor is in reality none other than the officer. He asks for the hand of the podesta's daughter Laurette in return for treating the alleged poisoning.

Around eighty composers replied to Offenbach's call for a score and after sorting them out twelve musicians remained that were actually given the libretto to work with. Like the first movement of his symphony, Bizet wrote a lively, syncopated overture. Meanwhile nineteen years old, in this first score for the musical theater Bizet proves that he is best whenever he makes fun of the weaknesses of grand opera and traditional comic opera. He knew where their problems lay. His models were obviously the operas buffas by Rossini and Donizetti, and some of his orchestra passages remind us of Carl Maria von Weber. His bizarre quartet "Voici l'omelette" is a fine little piece of uninhibited musical banter.

The jury, however, could not agree on a winning score and split the prize between two contestants: Bizet and his fellow student Alexandre Charles Lecocq, who also studied under Benoist and Halévy. A toss of the coin decided that Lecocq's work would be premiered first on 8 April 1857, and Bizet's work the next day. But after eight showings that followed each of the premieres, both pieces were forgotten.

Bizet knew, however, that Offenbach's style of bouffe was not where he saw his future. Lecocq (1832–1918) went on to become a popular composer of operettas. Bizet's one-act *Le Docteur miracle* did not see the stage again until 1951 when students performed it at the Paris Conservatory.

Notes

1. Taken from Joseph Wulf, *Musik im Dritten Reich* (Frankfurt am Main, 1966), 428.

2. *Der Konzertführer*, ed. A. Csampai and D. Holland (Reinbek, 1987), 445.

3. The condition of the original score, which consists of several different kinds of music paper, taken together with changes in the composer's handwriting and in his habits of notation, suggests that it did take him longer to write this symphony.

4. The conservatory's archive also contains two other piano arrangements that Bizet wrote as a candidate for the prize in 1856 and 1857: *Le Golfe de Baia* based on text by Alphonse de Lamartine and *Le Chanson de rouet* (Song of the Spinning Wheel).

5. Offenbach's call for pieces in *Le Figaro* of 17 July 1856. Taken from P. Walter Jacob, *Jacques Offenbach* (Reinbek, 1969), 66.

CHAPTER FOUR

Off to Rome for
Clovis and Clotilde, 1856–1859

Bizet perhaps used one of the free tickets he had won from the Prix de Rome competition to see Verdi's opera *La traviata*. Three years after its first showing, it was now premiering in Paris in 1856 at the *Théâtre Italien*. This theater played at the Salle Ventadour (formerly the site of the Opéra Comique) in Paris, performing works by Italian composers in Italian. This particular performance of *La traviata* would by no means have been an ordinary premiere: six years earlier, French censors had prohibited the mounting of a theater version of Alexandre Dumas Jr.'s *Lady of the Camellias*, the literary text on which *La traviata* is based.

Docteur miracle's success ushered Bizet into Paris's choice cultural circles. He was introduced to Gioachino Rossini, who since 1855 maintained homes both in Paris and in the suburb of Passy. When they met, Rossini's fame for *Barbiere di Siviglia* (The Barber of Seville, 1816) and *Guillaume Tell* (William Tell, 1829) was long established. The elderly composer had become a monument to himself, occasionally writing short pieces that he called "sins of old age," and hosting guests at his salon. An invitation to dine with the grand gourmet Rossini was a particularly coveted sign of social recognition. And naturally the composer was among those invited to opening nights at Offenbach's Bouffes-Parisiens. The Offenbach family also hosted Friday evening soirees, and as one of many pianists, Bizet often provided entertainment with his solid repertoire and competent improvising. Rossini, the old master of Italian opera buffa and grand opera, and Offenbach, Paris's German reviver

Théâtre Italien, drawing by Eugène Lami. *Steel engraving by C. Mottram*

of the musical theater, both encouraged Bizet to enter the Prix de Rome competition once again.

Meanwhile the jury included Hector Berlioz, despite the fact that thirty years previously he had failed to win the prize with his own cantata *La Mort d'Orphée*. In 1848 he had even ranted at the institution of the Prix de Rome itself, peeved particularly by the circumstance that the first assessment of submitted cantatas was undertaken by members of the academy regardless of their discipline and based on merely hearing the piece played on the piano:

> Six jury members from the music department can at least read the score and to some extent judge the skimpy and bungling piano performance, while the non-musical members of the academy cannot even do that. . . . In fairness I must say that since painters and engravers preside over music competitions, the musicians return the favor when judging painting, copper etching, and so on.[1]

In 1857 the text for the Académie des Beaux-Arts's Rome Prize cantata was a poem called *Clovis et Clotilde* written by Amédée Burion. Burion, apparently a railroad official, had already published texts in a variety of genres, including a school devotional booklet for the month of May[2] and, surprisingly, a libretto for the opera *Le Chant d'Antonia* by Victor Chéri, based on E. T. A. Hoffmann. Candidates for the prize were expected to compose their scores alone, but they did gather and socialize.

Hector Berlioz, photography by Nadar, about 1865. *Bibliothèque Nationale, Paris*

After some debate among the jury, Bizet was awarded the first prize for his score to the text. When we compare Bizet's music for *Clovis et Clotilde* (unfortunately the score he entered the first time he competed has never been found) to the cantata that Berlioz entered in 1827 (which was much more ambitious but nevertheless did not win), it looks as if here the young composer kept his eye on material needs as well as on Rome and took no risks in writing music that was sure to please nonmusical jurors. The piece sounds a bit like fashionable Verdi (especially the closing cadence of the reverent duet "Vers toi monte notre prière") and a bit like baritone verse à la Gounod (who incidentally loved the silly text),[3] but otherwise exhibits little novelty.

Being half an hour long, Bizet's work was somewhat longer than other winning pieces. It was shown on 2 October 1857, exactly three months after winning the prize, for the first, and for more than a century the only, time. *Clovis et Clotilde* tells the story of the Catholic princess of Burgundy, Clotilde (soprano), and her father Rémy (baritone) converting Clovis (tenor), first king of the Franks, to Christianity. In 486 Clovis had defeated the Roman official Syagrius in the battle at Soissons (one hundred kilometers northeast of Paris). In 1986, in celebration of the 1500th anniversary of the historical event, local music enthusiasts dug out Bizet's cantata and had renowned performers sing the original version at the cathedral of Soissons to commemorate the 150th anniversary of Bizet's birth.[4]

Gioachino Rossini, photograph by Nadar, about 1865

Just before Christmas in 1857, Georges Bizet and three other young winners of the prize (a painter, an architect, and an oboist who had also put music to the cantata text and won the "second" first prize) departed for Rome. It
was the first time that nineteen-year-old Bizet had ever left Paris. With him
he took letters of recommendation from Gounod, Michèle Enrico Carafa,[5]
and Rossini. "Mr. Bizet . . . is an exceptional person who deserves that you
and I do what we can for him," wrote Rossini to Felice Romani, Bellini's
most important libretto writer, who had also written texts for Donizetti's
L'elisir d'amore, Verdi's *Un giorno di regno*, and Rossini's own *Turco in Italia*.[6]
Rossini also explicitly mentioned *Le Docteur miracle*'s success.

Together with Charles Sellier, Joseph-Eugène Heim, and Charles Colin,
Bizet left Paris on 21 December. They probably took the train to Lyon. We
know that they spent Christmas in Avignon. Experiencing the countryside
and open nature for the first time, Bizet, the city boy, was deeply impressed.
He absorbed the hills and mountains of Provence and how the Rhône becomes ever more Mediterranean as it takes its course. The people spoke a
different language, not the French of the capital, but often pure Provençal. In
a village south of Avignon lived Frédéric Mistral, working on his epic poem
Mirèio (in the dialect of Provence) that was soon to become very popular
and later put to music by Gounod (*Mireille*, 1864). It seemed as if people in
Paris found the daily grind of urban progress growing dull and were keen to
discover not only remote exotic places, but unfamiliar places in their own
country as well.

"We took wonderful hikes. Mountains, rivers—nothing could stop us,"
wrote Bizet to his parents. "Heim takes no pity on my legs and thanks to him
I will probably lose quite a bit of weight. The spring is wonderful; the sun
shines and the sky is as blue as in Paris it is only in July. The trip is beautiful,
and if it weren't for the fact that I miss you so much, I'd be entirely happy.
Hector[7] was right to be so enthusiastic about his homeland. It is picturesque
and impressive and an artist simply must take advantage of it."[8]

Of course the four travelers, and particularly architect Heim, were also
interested in the many cultural monuments along the way. They visited
palaces, churches, and museums, stopped at the ancient arena at Orange,
and took a short detour to Nîmes before finally reaching Arles. More than
Sellier or Heim, Bizet especially was to be lastingly impressed by the spirit,
tongue, and manners of the people in that city. Unlike the painter Sellier,
he could not sit and immediately sketch his impressions on paper. But fifteen years later he composed music that was to become indelibly associated
with the name of the city and the nature of her Provençal surroundings and
inhabitants.

The group took the coach on to Salon, Aix, and Toulon. It was the first time Bizet had ever seen the sea. By year's end they had reached the border of Piedmont and Savoy, the Kingdom of Sardinia, which included Monaco and the city of Nice, that not until three years later were to become French in return for Napoleon III's assistance in uniting Italy as a nation.

In the second week of January 1858, having passed two further frontiers, the four young Frenchmen finally arrived in Florence, the capital of the grand duchy of Toscana, and were taken in by the place's wealth of art treasures. Bizet took an opportunity to hear Verdi's *I Lombardi alla prima crociata* sung in Italian. "Florence is a wonderful city! The museums hold the most beautiful items by Leonardo da Vinci, Tizian, etc. . . . It's paradise! There's so much life here, so much going on all the time, but sadly, no talent—not a musician, nor an author, not a painter, absolutely no one. It's peculiar to see such a famous country reduced to such decadence."[9]

On 27 January 1858, Jean-Victor Schnetz welcomed Bizet, Colin, Heim, and Sellier to Pincian Hill in Rome, where the Villa Medici had been French government property since 1803. Schnetz, a painter, was the current director of the French Academy in Rome. The post was awarded by the French government to a respected artist for a period of six years. One well-known former director had been Jean-Auguste-Dominique Ingres. The room assigned to Bizet for the first weeks of his stay had been decorated years ago by Horace Vernet (1789–1863) in Turkish style with Arabic characters. Among the other pensioners at the academy at the time was Félix Henri Giacomotti (1828–1909), who made a portrait of young Bizet before returning to Paris where he became known particularly for erotic pictures of women.

Later Gounod, who had also been a stipendiary at the Villa Medici, wrote: "Let us do all we can to maintain this noble sanctuary, where the young artist can develop and thrive, far from the trouble and travail that will beset him soon enough, and protected from the disdainful lure of lucre and the base triumphs of worthless and fleeting popularity."[10]

The villa's charm, the Eternal City, the Roman zest for life, and particularly, Rome's women all fascinated Georges Bizet. For two years he would live at the Villa Medici, studying and working. The academy in Paris awaited so-called *envois*, namely, proof of progress.

In the spring Bizet and other awardees made excursions to the mountains, surrounding cities, and the sea. He became an avid swimmer but neglected his fragile health. Head colds, a sore throat, and symptoms of rheumatism occasionally frustrated his enterprising spirit and drive.

As early as on the journey to Rome itself he had written home to his mother: "I'm fine, except for a common cold that I brought with me from

Paris. It's stubborn as the devil. Every night I drink a cup of warm milk and nutmeg: You see, I remember your remedy."[11]

Bizet's letters from Rome, addressed almost exclusively to his mother, are the only accounts we have from the artist himself that give us any reliable hint of his personality for any continuous period of time. His letters are spontaneous and clear; in one postscript he says outright that he never rereads what he has written before putting it in the mail. He was not yet twenty when he left home for the first time and thanks to winning the award, he now lived with other young artists in a splendid place and at first entirely free of everyday worries. He would have had little time and no inclination to elaborate any further thoughts than his daily impressions. Even much-respected Mina Curtiss calls Bizet's correspondence from Rome "schoolboy letters."[12]

"There is much to admire, but also much that is disillusioning. Bad taste is poisoning Italy. The country is entirely oblivious to art; either they have never heard of Rossini, Mozart, Weber, Paer,[13] and Cimarosa, or they belittle or have forgotten them. How sad! The theater is closed during Lent, but then they have extravagant religious celebrations during Holy Week . . . these ridiculous Madonna figures under every street lamp. They hang their laundry out the windows to dry and leave dung on the Piazza. . . . I'd love to show you the charming view from my window for just one moment."[14]

During the course of their scholarship stay in Rome, winners of the Prix de Rome were allowed to compete for the Rodrigues Award that would bring them another 1500 francs. Georges Bizet was interested in the money and less in the honor or the art involved in winning it. He wanted it to finance a detour through Switzerland that he planned to make when traveling to Germany. He was also already thinking of how he might secure his existence as a composer. In his room at the Villa Medici he thus began in February 1858 to write his first "Italian" music, namely *Te Deum*.

In mid-April he reported back to Paris: "My *Te Deum* is almost finished, I just need yet to orchestrate it. I can think of nothing else. Sometimes I like it; sometimes I think it's horrible. One thing is certain, and that is that I am not made for writing church music. And I would rather not write a mass. I plan to write an Italian opera in three acts; I like that better."[15]

Bizet's *Te Deum* score for soprano and tenor solos, a mixed choir, and an orchestra—his only religious work at all—is clearly marked by what he took to be Italian. It follows pompous, glorifying works more than it resembles meditative French *Te Deum* music by Charpentier, Gossec, or Berlioz. He emphasizes the Latin words of the first verse, however, in a very French way: "Te Deúm laudamús." This almost pounding syncopation right at the beginning and the indulgent cantilenas for both solo voices are clearly in operatic style. In other words, just like Rossini's *Stabat mater* that premiered at an opera house,[16] what we have here is not liturgical, but stylized church music. Winton Dean may not have considered that distinction when calling it "a wretched work . . . music of the kind that seems to presuppose Blackpool pier and somebody's silver tuba band."[17]

The soprano solo "Tu Rex gloriae, Christe" with its surprising trombone solo (perhaps a bow to the "Tuba mirum" from Mozart's *Requiem?*) and insistent pointed rhythm has its very own strong sound. The obligatory fugue, on the other hand, written for the text "Fiat misericordia" is less inspired. Bizet of course understood the purpose and had mastered the technique of polyphone forms, but he did not need them for what he had to say. Although he competed against only one other composer, Bizet did not win the Rodrigues Award that had been founded and financed by banker and patron Édouard Rodrigues-Henriques, a cousin of Hannah Léonie Halévy (nee Rodrigues-Henriques). His *Te Deum* was not premiered until 1971, in Berlin.

About a year later, Bizet clearly explained his relationship to church music: "People ask me to compose religious music: Well then, I write religious pieces, but they are godless religious pieces. I've been thinking of Horace's *Carmen Saeculare* [Secular Hymn] for a long time: There is nothing more beautiful than ancient Latin."[18] Also known as the "Song of the Ages," Quintus Horatius Flaccus's hymn celebrates Augustinian Rome and Roman gods. Bizet felt more drawn to ancient Rome than to the papal city where he lived. But he never did set Horace's poem to music.

Notes

1. Hector Berlioz, *Mémoires*, trans. into German by Elly Elles (Leipzig, 1967), 101f.

2. *Mois de Marie à l'usage des maisons d'education* (Paris, 1853).

3. Charles Gounod, "Lettres à Georges Bizet," *Revue de Paris* 6 (1899): 679.

4. Documented on a CD with Montserrat Caballé under the direction of Jean-Claude Casadeus.

5. M. E. Carafa (1787–1872) was a productive, Italian opera composer who lived in Paris as of 1827.

6. Letter dated 15 December 1857. Taken from Luigi Rognoni's *Gioachino Rossini* (Turin, 1977), 309.

7. Hector Gruyer, one of his father's pupils.

8. Georges Bizet, *Lettres (1850–1875): Choisies et présentées par Claude Glayman* (Paris, 1989), 48.

9. Bizet, *Lettres*, 53.

10. Charles Gounod, *Mémoires d'un artiste* (Paris, 1896), 311.

11. Bizet, *Lettres*, 49.

12. Mina Curtiss, *Bizet and His World* (New York, 1958), 51.

13. Ferdinando Paer (1771–1839), an Italian opera composer (*Leonora*, 1804) who worked in Paris.

14. Bizet, *Lettres*, 60, 64f.

15. Bizet, *Lettres*, 63.

16. At the Théâtre Italien in Paris in 1842.

17. Dean, *Bizet* (London, 1975), 157.

18. Bizet, *Lettres*, 125.

CHAPTER FIVE

Instead of a Mass, an Opera Buffa, 1859

Having had no luck with his religious piece and eager to write his first opera, Bizet simply ignored the fact that the academy in Paris expected his *envoi*, the proof of his progress, to be a mass and contemplated doing Felice Romani's *Parisina* libretto for which Donizetti had already written music. But despite recommendation from Rossini, Bizet probably did not meet Romani and soon dropped that plan. He began searching libraries and shops, in new and used books, for a good idea. He came up with *Don Procopio*.

"I sought and found an Italian farce in *Don Pasquale* style. . . . I am clearly made to write buffa music and fully devoted to it. I went through every bookshop in Rome and two hundred texts. In Italy they write exclusively for Verdi, Mercadante, and Pacini. For others they simply use translations of French operas. Disregarding copyrights, they take a piece by Scribe, translate, and put their name to it without changing a word."[1]

The plot for Carlo Cambiaggio's *Don Procopio* libretto, which Vincenzo Fioravanti and Giuseppe Mosca had already once put to music for Trieste, reminds of the story from Domenico Cimarosa's *Il matrimonio segreto*: In order to secure the family's estate, Don Andronico, an old miser, seeks to marry his moneyed niece to a man of his liking. But the girl falls in love with a young military officer. With the help of her mother and brother she gets her uncle's choice, Don Procopio, to find her so obnoxious that he willingly retreats.

Bizet skipped using an orchestra prelude to get the piece going, starting instead right off with a choir singing of rural life at Uncle Andronico's estate. The introduction's weave of solos and choir parts, instrumentation, and dramaturgy all display Bizet's typical style and skill at evoking stage atmospheres that enhance the story—an art that he was to bring to perfection in *Carmen*. His Italian (that he had already begun learning in Paris) was elegant and pointed, and he also brought in the tone of his own symphony. In fact, Don Odoardo enters the stage to a march taken directly from the symphony's last movement (see music sample on the bottom of page 20).

Remarkably, and to our amusement, Bizet also cleverly tried to make act 1 of *Don Procopio* end with a concerted grand finale format similar to Verdi's *La traviata*. But on the other hand he wanted to win over his audience by having a lighthearted stretto directly follow the text "*Che scuro labirinto! Che strana confusione!*" Rossini's *Barber of Seville* was unmistakably the model for it. Act 2 gets an obvious dramatic touch from a trio by the bride's uncle, brother, and suitor. It is embedded in entirely conventional music like Odoardo's tenor serenade that rings of Donizetti ("*Sulle piume dell'amore*"), despite the unusual guitar, mandolin, and double English horn accompaniment. "All I do, and it will please Papa, is Italian music. What else can you do with Italian lyrics? The sky and climate affect me, too," he wrote home in late January 1859,[2] sending the score, his *envoi*, to Paris somewhat later. In recognition of the piece's qualities, the first response from Paris was encouraging: "Overall, the work is marked by a light and brilliant tone and young audacious style, which are valuable features for the comical genre, as the composer particularly points out. These are promising qualities. . . ."[3] Bizet was relieved and felt confirmed in his choice of genres. While he had been working on his opera buffa in Rome, in Paris Offenbach had taken an important step for the future of light musical theater by premiering the first version of *Orphée aux enfers* (Orpheus in the Underworld).

In Italy young Bizet had many plans. He wanted to write another symphony and noted themes for operas, but then discarded them. Shakespeare fascinated him, and he thought of doing Hamlet, or Esmeralda, in other words, a "Notre Dame" opera à la Victor Hugo with a gypsy heroine or a buoyant "Don Quixote." He also considered using Molière's *L'Amour peintre* for an opera comique, and felt drawn to one of E. T. A. Hoffmann's tales as well. To his mother he wrote: "Get tales by Hoffmann from the library and read *Martin the Master Cooper and His Journeymen* [from the collection *The Serapion Brethren*]. I'd like to make a piece in three acts out of this story . . . the 'singer contest' would make quite an original scene and have a certain effect."[4] At that time he could not have already seen Wagner's *Tannhäuser and the Singers' Contest at Wartburg Castle*, although he would have been familiar with parts of it. But eventually the young Frenchman living on Rome's sunny Pincian Hill dropped the idea of musically working out E. T. A. Hoffmann's *Martin* from the dank cellars of quaint Nuremberg.

Georges Bizet, painting by Félix-Henri Giacomotti, 1860.
Bibliothèque Nationale, Paris

Le Tonnelier de Nuremberg, like many other titles that Bizet mentioned he was considering as opera material, found its way into lists of his works and spawned the legend that he had written many never-completed operas. Winton Dean counted as many as thirty-one of them, although no. 22 is oddly some sort of "Caucasian material" for which Dean could specify neither title, nor author, nor source.

In Rome Bizet still practiced the piano and gave piano concerts, generally for other stipendiaries and social events, where he was understandably a more accommodating entertainer than the students of painting and architecture. His mentor Schnetz valued him for that. But for Bizet the piano, the starting point of his musical career, soon became less and less an instrument for concert giving, and more and more a tool for shaping his idea of how an orchestra must sound, and for exploring the works of other composers.

During his stay Bizet apparently only wrote three pieces for the piano, each just three minutes long. The first of these *Trois Esquisses musicale* (Three Musical Sketches), a *Ronde Turque* (Turkish rondo), strikes an "exotic" note, perhaps inspired by the interior decoration of his room at the villa.

In style, the Turkey that Bizet conjures up here has nothing to do with Mozart's *Rondo Alla Turca*, nor with janissary music. Bizet strives for magical, oriental sentiment, only to ultimately contrast it with a fugato that seems out of place. The little trilogy's *Caprice* flounces the minstrel style from his symphony.

From his mother's letters and from other persons from Paris that visited the Villa Medici, Bizet heard of Charles Gounod's success in premiering Faust on 19 March 1859. Following *Nonne sanglante* in 1854, in 1858 Gounod's music for a stage adaptation of Molière's *Le Médecin malgré lui* had been mediocre. Bizet also heard that his friend Hector Gruyer had disappointed in the title role. Gounod's *Faust* was a new kind of opera: so-called *drame lyrique* that combined the spoken dialogue and dramaturgical stringency of opera comique with the artistic expressiveness of grand opera. Bizet was soon studying *Faust* very carefully. He sensed that the musical theater was moving from opera comique to grand opera and that it was significant for his own development.

The scholarship winners worked at their arts, enjoying Mediterranean life and worrying little about politics, although Rome found itself at the very epicenter of cataclysmic political change. In January 1858 an Italian, Felice Orsini, had tried to assassinate Napoleon III. The event convinced the emperor to intervene more decisively in unifying Italy as a nation. When he himself had still been an emigrant, he had pledged to work toward freedom for the neighbor country controlled by Habsburg. In early May 1859, France came to the assistance of Sardinia-Piedmont and declared war on Austria. The Austrians vacated Milan; Habsburg's dukes fled from Florence and Modena. Finally, on 24 June 1859 at Solferino in the province of Mantua Emperor Franz Joseph I was defeated in the bloodiest battle of the century. But ultimately Italy was unified without the help of Napoleon III. The French emperor had simultaneously supported the interests of the pope. Now Bizet lived in a city that had become the capital of the Papal State of Pius IX (Rome was not

Battle at Solferino. *Painting by Carlo Bossoli*

Italy's capital until 1871), although the majority of its citizens would rather have seen Vittorio Emanuele from Savoy as their king.

The disclosed aspects of Bizet's political opinion during that time (and at others) are rather ambivalent. On the one hand, he was a Frenchman. On the other hand, he was a freethinking individualist and impressed by the charisma of his Italian colleague Giuseppe Verdi, whose name had become a slogan: "V. E. R. D. I.—Vittorio Emanuele Re d'Italia." In September 1859, forty-five-year-old Verdi was elected as representative of Parma and received by Vittorio Emanuele in Turin. Bizet disliked Verdi's most recent opera, *Un ballo in maschera* (A Masked Ball): "Wretched! The singers, the orchestra, the furnishings—Awful!!!"[5] Perhaps Bizet was still strongly biased for Auber's conventional style. Auber's grand opera *Gustav III* that uses a libretto by Scribe to tell the same story of a masked ball had been until recently a much-played hit in Paris.

Bizet's assessment of the successful Italian composer was immature and ambivalent. He recognized the importance and vivacity of Verdi's operas, even emulated them, but also envied Verdi for his easy disrespect for tradition. Like Wagner, Verdi was free of institutions constantly evaluating his art; Bizet had to always please the academy. An early letter from Rome contains an odd remark: "More than ever, I'm convinced that Mozart and Rossini are the two greatest musicians. I admire the talents of Beethoven and Meyerbeer; but I feel naturally more drawn to pure and simple art than to dramatic passion. The same holds for painting: Raphael is like Mozart; Meyerbeer seems like Michelangelo. But don't take me too seriously; on the contrary, I have come to the point where I acknowledge that Verdi is a dedicated genius on the most wretched path ever taken."[6] Soon thereafter it would hardly have occurred to him to compare Meyerbeer with Michelangelo and Beethoven.

Unexpectedly, March 1860 bitterly disappointed Bizet. The conservative formalists at the Paris Academy, who had expected the *envoi* to be a mass, had meanwhile gained the upper hand and now scolded Bizet for sending *Don Procopio*: "We must admonish Mr. Bizet for writing an opera buffa instead of the

Giuseppe Verdi, photograph by Nadar, about 1860. *Bibliothèque Nationale, Paris*

obligatory mass. We remind him that the most spirited of beings discover that indispensable style without which a work can never be enduring, by struggling with the interpretation of both sublime works and simple pieces."[7] Bizet took the warning signed by Ambroise Thomas to heart and conformed. After all, he did want to live from composing and for starters that was only possible when backed by established members of the academy. Auber, the director of the academy, stowed away the score for *Don Procopio* and forgot it. It was lost among the numerous pages of music left unorganized when he died.

Bizet never saw a performance of his first opera. Much later music scholar and opera librarian Charles Malherbe rediscovered it. He took Bizet's opera buffa and made a kind of French opera comique out of it by adding recitatives. It was shown for the first time in 1906 in Monte Carlo. Malherbe also composed an entire *Intermezzo sinfonico* based on Bizet motifs. *Don Procopio* was not shown in its original Italian form until 1908 when it played at the Teatro Costanzi in Rome, starring Amelita Galli Curci and Giuseppe de Luca. The piece had been translated into German, but was never performed.[8] Its first recording was in the Soviet Union in 1962, having been translated into Russian. All of these versions plus three later additional recordings sung in Italian and a live recording in French from 1948 (that was not available until much later) were based on the questionable performance material that Malherbe had assembled. To this day no one has edited Bizet's original text.

Notes

1. Georges Bizet, *Lettres (1850–1875): Choisies et présentées par Claude Glayman* (Paris, 1989), 67.

2. Bizet, *Lettres*, 87.

3. Bizet, *Lettres*, 115.

4. Bizet, *Lettres*, 103.

5. Bizet, *Lettres*, 117.

6. Bizet, *Lettres*, 73.

7. Bizet, *Lettres*, 125.

8. It was translated by Wilhelm Hüttemann (Ahns Text-Bibliothek No. 133, Cologne, n.d.).

CHAPTER SIX

Vasco da Gama and Roma, 1859–1860

In the summer of 1859 Bizet and fellow students traveled to the "Kingdom of the Two Sicilies," Naples and Pompeii, stopping in Terracina on the Gulf of Gaeta on their way back to Rome. Every operagoer in France knew the name of this city about one hundred kilometers south of Rome because Terracina was the setting for Auber's *Fra Diavolo*. The ancient city on the sea lies near Cape Circeo, the legendary realm of the goddess of magic, Circe. Like many musicians before him, Bizet, too, was fascinated by the setting for that episode from Homer's *Odyssey*. As a fourteen-year-old, at the Comédie-Française he had seen François Ponsard's dramatic version of the story to stage music by Gounod. Bizet now composed a symphonic ode, a kind of dramatic cantata on the theme. Félicien David's *Le Désert* was one of the most popular pieces of this kind. Although orientalism had already long been observable in French painting, David was the first to bring oriental sounds and tunes to French music. He had authentic firsthand impressions to go by: running from political persecution, from 1833 to 1835 he had traversed the Near East under occasionally rather adventurous circumstances.

In thus nodding to tradition, Bizet hoped to regain favor with the aging gentlemen in Paris—"Reber[1] is dumb, Berlioz absent, Auber asleep, Carafa and Clapisson[2] listen (alas!)."[3] Of the last two Bizet thought very little. The letter Carafa had given him on his way turned out to be anything but a recommendation. And Bizet's parody on Clapisson's style of composing that he had already tried out and performed on the piano in Paris and called *L'Enterrement de Clapisson* (Clapisson's Funeral) was said to have heartily

45

amused soirée goers at the Villa Medici. Nonetheless, in 1854, when electing new members for the academy, Clapisson was preferred to Berlioz. His rather shallow opera *La Fanchonette* (1856) was a pronounced success with the audience.

But having completed just a few outlines for *Ulysse et Circe*, Bizet stopped working on it. After returning to Rome he had borrowed *The Odyssey* from the library at the Villa Medici, a collection of works that he often used, studied it, and found it impossible to write music for. He remained fascinated by ancient epic, however, and a symphonic ode to Christopher Columbus by Félicien David gave him a new idea. Bizet's hero was to be a seafarer and discoverer from the fifteenth century: Vasco da Gama. The literary model was a Portuguese Renaissance poem by Luís Vaz de Camões based on Homer and Vergil and called *Os Lusiadas*. He was, however, unhappy with the text

Antoine-Louis Clapisson, 1866. *Roger-Viollet, Paris*

for it written by Louis Delâtre, a French writer living in Rome, and decided to write his own version.

The work recounts Vasco da Gama's journey from Portugal to East India. The seafarers battle a storm whipped up by a giant named Adamastor, sung by six basses. But the only part of the work that Bizet later still found valuable was a bolero for the officer Léonard (soprano).

Here Bizet did not attain the level of musical expression that he had already once achieved. As a musical dramatist he needed motivated stage action. Meanwhile his plans for writing for the orchestra had matured. "My thoughts always turn to my symphony and I am almost ready to write the closing movement. I hope to move forward with the third movement, while I have yet to complete the second."[4] Note that here he writes to his mother about the first symphony he now has on his mind; he does not count the one he had written five years earlier.

While France began intractable involvement in Indochina, in 1860 the musical scene of Paris debated over three concerts of his own works that Richard Wagner conducted at the Italian Theater. The prelude to *Tristan und Isolde* met with perplexity. Auber, Berlioz (whom Wagner had given a copy of the score for *Tristan*), Gounod, Meyerbeer, and Ernest Reyer all sat in the audience. Wagner received Camille Saint-Saëns at his salon and went to visit Rossini. "Tout Paris," including the imperial family, spoke of the Saxon composer. Reyer soon began composing a Nordic *Sigurd* opera that was not premiered until twenty years later, after Wagner's *Ring* had already dealt with the same material. Thirty-six-year-old Reyer had an affinity for the German tradition and admired Carl Maria von Weber, but at the time he had made a name for himself with "exotic works" like the *Sakountala* ballet and the oriental symphony *Le Sélam*.

At that time, and still in Rome, Bizet was thus working on at least one movement for a symphony. He had ideas for three further movements, had outlined and begun and then discarded some of them, and put them aside. He did not complete them and make them available for performance until much later.

In the fall of 1859, Ernest Guiraud won the Prix de Rome. The news that his dear friend and esteemed fellow student had won the award, and the prospect of having his company, strengthened Bizet's resolve to request that his own stipend be extended; to get it he was willing—against Gounod's advice—to forgo the scheduled stay in Germany. Guiraud arrived in Rome in the spring of 1860. During his stay at the Villa Medici, Guiraud, too, would write an Italian opera: *Gli avventurieri*.

That summer Bizet and Guiraud took a long trip to northern Italy. Diaries from that journey with remarks on cathedrals, church organs, and brothel visits found their way from the private drawers of Mina Curtiss to the *Bibliothéque nationale*. The two young men saw Perugia, Assisi, Pesaro, Rossini's place of birth, Ravenna, and Padua, reaching Venice in early September. In a letter to his mother on his way from Rimini (which remained papal for merely a few more weeks) to Habsburg Venice, Bizet wrote: "I have a symphony in mind that I would like to call 'Rome, Venice, Florence, and Naples.' It all goes wonderfully together: 'Venice' will be my andante, 'Rome' my first movement, 'Florence' my scherzo, and 'Naples' my finale; I believe it's a novel idea."[5]

In *Roma*, as the work came to be known and that Bizet later called "my symphony" (although it has also misleadingly been called a suite),[6] Bizet worked out his impressions of Italy. Tchaikovsky, too, distinguished between his large symphonies and his suites that were no less symphonic. *Roma* documents Bizet's development as a composer during his stay abroad. Its second movement (*Allegretto vivace*, scherzo)—that we know was written at the Villa Medici, while the other movements were completed in Paris—is well wrought, but like the third, slow movement it, too, is only modestly novel. The first movement is mature and truly symphonic; in following great models it begins with a calm *Andante* and then becomes *Allegro agitato*. The sound of the horn quartet can be placed somewhere between Mendelssohn's *Midsummer Night's Dream* nocturne, Weber's *Marksman*, and Wagner's *Tannhäuser*:

The later engraved score for *Roma* contained only one programmatic subtitle, indicating the last movement as *Carnival*. But any association with Mendelssohn's *Italian Symphony* or Berlioz's brilliant *Roman Carnival* takes us in the entirely wrong direction. Despite the prescribed *Allegro vivacissimo* the movement contains no unleashed gaiety, but is instead marked by a peculiarly choral-like thought that seems to evolve from some entirely different context.

Gustav Mahler liked *Roma* and performed it in Vienna in 1901. Eduard Hanslick said, "One can hardly say that this work displays originality or a wealth of innovation; but it does have charming, witty, even dazzling parts

Bizet returning to Paris, drawing by Gaston Planté, 1860. *Bibliothèque Nationale, Paris*

with thoroughly delightful instrumentation . . . as if, at times, an opera scene were being played behind closed curtains."[7] Later a self-critical Bizet said to Saint-Saëns regarding his symphonic ambitions: "I'm just not made to write symphonies. I need the stage. Without the stage I can't do anything."[8]

While in Venice, Bizet had received a letter from his mother saying that she was quite ill and depressed. He replied on 5 September 1860: "I wait so impatiently for your next letter. If you have the slightest desire that I return immediately, say so openly, and if you wish, I will take the next train."[9] Deeply worried, at the end of the month he returned sooner than planned to his family in Paris.

Somewhere along the way Georges Bizet must have met twenty-six-year-old but already famous physicist and inventor of the battery, Gaston Planté. He was probably also on his way back to Paris, perhaps returning from his home region of the Pyrenees, and drew the musician wearing a hat and holding an umbrella. The two were possibly already fleetingly acquainted: Planté's younger brother Francis had been greatly admired as best of the piano class under Marmontel and, though a year Bizet's junior, had already won the first prize in 1850. He went on to become an outstanding performer, particularly for works by Chopin and Schumann.

Notes

1. Napoléon Henri Reber (1807–1880), professor for harmonics and later for composition as Halévy's successor at the conservatory.

2. Antoine-Louis Clapisson (1808–1866), violinist and composer of operettas.

3. Dean, *Bizet* (London, 1975), 26.

4. George Bizet, *Lettres (1850–1875): Choisies et présentées par Claude Glayman* (Paris, 1989), 122.

5. Bizet, *Lettres*, 134.

6. For a long time *Roma* was given the subtitle "Suite No. 3 for Orchestra." Suite Nos. 1 and 2 were music from *Carmen* and *L'Arlésienne* that was later, respectively, called the "First Suite" of each work.

7. Eduard Hanslick, *Aus neuer und neuester Zeit* (Berlin, 1900), 77f.

8. Charles-Camille Saint-Saëns, *Musikalische Reminizenzen*, trans. into German by Eva Zimmermann (Leipzig, 1978), 202.

9. Bizet, *Lettres*, 136.

CHAPTER SEVEN

Back in the Capital, 1861–1862

Georges Bizet had been away from Paris for almost three years. Now, as an adult and a professional composer, he had to find his way through a network of important contacts, collegial relationships, patrons, and intrigues, from casual acquaintances to concert managers to publishers.

In 1861, Eugène Scribe died, the great poet for the theater and preceptor of French opera libretto. For decades he would influence the style of many subsequent writers. Two weeks after his death, the performance of Richard Wagner's *Tannhäuser*, reworked especially to meet the demands of the opera in Paris, escalated to one of the most discussed opera events of the century. To suit Parisian taste, Wagner had added a ballet (the *Venusberg Bacchanal*) to the opera (already once shown in 1845 in Dresden), but he also jolted the audience by having the dance directly follow the overture.

Legend has it that in May 1861 Franz Liszt was a guest at the home of Halévy who gave Bizet an opportunity to demonstrate his piano skill to the great virtuoso. Liszt is said to have praised the young French musician and found him as good as himself and his son-in-law Hans von Bülow.[1] Any such encounter is more likely to have taken place at the home of instrument builder Érard on the rue du Mail, where Liszt stayed when he visited Paris and where Bizet went occasionally.

At their home on the rue de la Tour d'Auvergne, Bizet's father and their maid Marie Reiter cared for Madame Bizet. Marie, just one year older than the son of the family, consoled him during his difficult time after returning from Italy, when he learned that his mother had not much longer to live.

Aimée Bizet died on 8 September 1861, aged forty-six. Meanwhile, Georges had a relationship going with Marie. About his earlier relationships with women there exist only a few immature comments from his letters from Rome; naturally, erotic adventures would had not have been topical in reports to his mother. In the late spring of 1862 Marie left Paris in a state of advanced pregnancy to stay for a while in Alsace, her home region. But she soon returned with her newborn son and resumed her work at the household of widower Bizet and his son.

Little Jean Reiter was passed off as the son of the elder Monsieur Bizet and raised by the family. It is said that Marie Reiter kept her secret until her son was sixty years old and then, on her deathbed, told him that he was the offspring of the meanwhile world-famous composer of *Carmen*, and not his half brother.

Back in Paris from Rome, Georges Bizet began working on his next music for the stage. A successful team of writers, Jules Barbier and Michel Carré, who had written text for Gounod's *Faust*, had also written a libretto called *La Guzla de l'Émir*. The *gusla* is a one-stringed instrument played by wandering southeast European rhapsodists. A piece branded as that promised to be mysteriously exotic, though not at all authentic, but that bothered no one in Paris, as long as the entertainment was good. As early as 1828, Johann Wolfgang von Goethe had written: "Not long ago, the French . . . seized foreign ways of writing. . . . But the newest and strangest phenomenon is that they now even come wearing masks of foreign nations and pleasantly fool us with foisted works. . . . We noticed that the word 'gusla' conceals the name of Gazul. . . . Monsieur Mérimée cannot blame us for claiming that he is the author behind the gusla and Clara Gazul's theater."[2]

Just as the *Theater of Clara Gazul* (published in 1825 as the alleged writing of a girl who had escaped a monastery, the daughter of a Spanish actress and a Moor) was in reality a hoax written by Prosper Mérimée, like Macpherson's fictitious *Ossian*, the Illyrian *Guzla* ballads (allegedly "collected in Dalmatia, Bosnia, Croatia, and Herzegovina" and then edited by one Hyacinthe Maglanowich) were also entirely products of Mérimée's pen. As an editor and interpreter of Spanish and Russian literature, Prosper Mérimée had considerable influence on the taste of contemporary French readers. In 1830 in Granada he had heard from the mother of the later French empress Eugénie the story of a former soldier who out of unrequited love had murdered a gypsy woman. Mérimée retold the story in his short novel *Carmen* (1847).

Bizet's *La Guzla de l'Émir* was planned as an opera comique that actually had a real chance of being performed at the house of the same name because governmental financial support for the Opéra Comique was linked to the condition that it played works of winners of the Prize of Rome. Bizet also now assisted Charles Gounod at rehearsals and in producing the piano score and copies of Gounod's latest work, *La Reine de Saba*, which was also based on a libretto by Carré and Barbier.

In March the next year, Jacques Fromental Halévy died at the age of sixty-three while working on his opera called *Noé*. At first Belgian composer François Auguste Gevaert was commissioned to complete the score, but then Halévy's widow turned the task over to Bizet. But for the present Bizet was more occupied with his own works and with liberating himself from his teacher's style. He also had to keep in mind that the academy was still waiting for a third *envoi*. Having reprimanded him for *Don Procopio* and approved of his "seafaring" cantata, the academy now expected something symphonic. Bizet probably intended to make *La Guzla de l'Émir* his fourth envoi. He took the completed scherzo from his *Roma Symphony* and added a funeral march in F minor (that can be seen as related to the death of his mother) and then wrote a concert overture called *La Chasse d'Ossian*, modeled after Mendelssohn's *Hebrides Overture (Fingal's Cave)* based on the Fingal and Ossian saga. Bizet's works were performed at the academy; the scherzo alone was repeated at a separate private performance.

At the time, the only institution in Paris that regularly offered symphony concerts was a society that had grown out of the *Société des Jeunes Artistes*

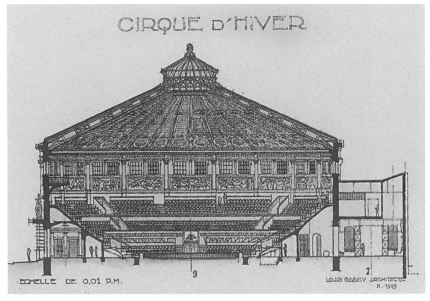

Cross-section of the Cirque d'Hiver

du Conservatoire and that beginning in1861 held concerts for classical music at the *Cirque d'Hiver* (Winter Circus), directed by conductor Jules Étienne Pasdeloup. There anyone could inexpensively hear the symphonic repertoire that was standard for the times, especially Haydn and Mozart, Beethoven, Weber, and Mendelssohn. Young contemporary French composers were given an opportunity. Pasdeloup presented Bizet's Roman scherzo (without the funeral march) between Mozart's E-flat major symphony (KV 543) and Beethoven's music for *Egmont*. The score for Bizet's Ossian Overture, most likely a compulsory assignment made to please the elderly members of the academy, has been lost.

Jules Étienne Pasdeloup. *Bibliothèque Nationale, Paris*

All of this enhanced Bizet's reputation but did not bring him much money for the future. His five-year scholarship grant was running out. To improve his finances, he could have become a successful piano teacher, but it did not harmonize well with the image of the opera composer that he wanted to project. He preferred to assist a colleague at premiering the latter's newest opera.

The challenge was to produce Ernest Reyer's *Érostrate* (Herostratus) which arts-minded casino concessionaire Édouard Bénazet had ordered for the first opera season at the new theater in Baden-Baden. Bizet hoped that Bénazet would commission him, too, to write an opera. He perhaps thought of composing music for a text on Russian tsar Ivan the Terrible that Gounod had left unused. Bizet continued working diligently in Paris, even after Reyer had left for the noble little spa town in Germany. He followed him to Baden-Baden later, where he also saw a performance of Hector Berlioz's new opera *Béatrice et Béndedict* that had been premiered on 9 August 1862 (incidentally not, as has often been claimed, to inaugurate the new theater). Bénazet found it too risky to immediately mount another contemporary French opera. For that reason, three days earlier they had shown Conradin Kreutzer's reliable *Nachtlager in Granada* (Night Camp in Granada).

Berlioz's adaptation of William Shakespeare's *Much Ado about Nothing* marked the aesthetic end of opéra comique, exhibiting all the signs of the genre's crisis. Its brilliant, witty, sophisticated music (with spoken dialogue, a tradition in opéra comique) overpowered all the needs of the theater, leaving little left to be comical. For not quite twenty-four-year-old Bizet that theater evening in Baden-Baden was surely a memorable experience.

In October the academy issued its verdict on *La Guzla*: "If this work still displays a little too much of the recondite and a certain tendency to sacrifice vocal interest to richness of accompaniment, we are happy again to recognize that loftiness of sentiment, vivacity of style, and certainty of execution, in a word, those serious qualities of which M. Bizet has already given proof."[3]

Finally, in early February 1863, *Vasco da Gama* was performed for a select audience at the academy for the first (and only) time. Critics from the *Revue des deux mondes* are said to have complained (and rightly so) that Bizet's piece closely resembled Félicien David's *Columbus* cantata. The young composer, who had now made a certain name for himself in Paris, was probably not struck all too hard by the criticism as he was now concentrating on his plans for the theater.

Meanwhile, winter had set in and Bizet's ambitious work not only on *Guzla*, but also on arrangements that he prepared for other colleagues led him to belittle frequent colds and infections. Some have assumed that he might even have had diphtheria. But in the end it was national politics and events in Italy that led him to retract *La Guzla de l'Émir*, although preparations for premiering it had already begun at the Opéra Comique. Léon Carvalho, a former baritone from just that stage, was the director of the Théâtre Lyrique at Place du Châtelet that later became the Théâtre Sarah Bernhardt and today is the Théâtre de la Ville. He had just been blessed with governmental subsidies on the condition that he show works by winners of the Prize of Rome.

It had been a decision of the new minister of the arts, who in July 1862 had laid the cornerstone for the sumptuous new Paris Opera, the Palais Garnier. Alexandre Graf Colonna-Walewski (1810–1868) was an illegitimate son of Napoleon I and a Polish countess. He had been the secretary of state but resigned from his office over Napoleon III's inconsistent stand on the unification of Italy; but now he naturally wanted to make a name for himself at his new post. Never again was there a comparable culturally political coup, namely, the governmental subsidizing of only those opera composers of whom the state approved.

The work to be subsidized had to be the first opera of the prize winner in question. Bizet's *Le Docteur miracle* counted as an operetta; *Don Procopio* was

Léon Carvalho

not considered French opera, nor had it ever been performed. Thus Bizet saw his chance: Carvalho offered him a text that he found fascinating and that allowed him to make his debut as an opera composer without adhering to the formal restrictions of the comique tradition. The libretto that Michel Carré had written in collaboration with Eugène Cormon (a pseudonym for the well-known opera stage director Pierre-Étienne Piestre) was *Leïla*.

Originally, *Leïla* also included spoken dialogue, but Carvalho decided that he wanted music for the entire piece. It had to be premiered in six months, because Carvalho wanted a modern production to show alongside Mozart's *Figaro*.

Posterity has never gotten to hear *La Guzla de l'Émir* as written by Bizet; he apparently destroyed the material although it was complete and ready for performance. Parts of it found their way into other of his works—perhaps into music for the *Leïla* libretto. The text for *Guzla* was not again put to music until ten years later, and then by Théodore Dubois, a church musician who had won the Prix de Rome in 1861.

Parisian audiences remained fond of exotic stories. *Salammbô*, Flaubert's novel about Carthage, was a best-seller. The accurate description of distant lands was irrelevant; fantasies and clichés were sufficient for success. Society gloated over peculiar figures and cultures, in part fancifully admiring them, but in part also wallowing in condescendence. The *Grande Nation*, still active in various colonial undertakings, not only sought diversion in the idyllic, but also confirmation of its own progressive grandeur in light of the strange customs of other peoples and what were considered lower forms of civilization. Painting in particular did not stop at describing the atmosphere of certain milieus. A picture by Henri Levy, just two years Bizet's junior, shows "Bonaparte at the Great Mosque of Cairo" bringing *illumination* to the people.

The French opera's roots in orientalism go back to *Gulistan* and *Azemia* by Nicolas Dalayrac (1753–1809). In 1862 Félicien David's *Lalla-Roukh* had been a huge hit at the Opéra Comique. It was shown more than one hundred times within one year. The text by Carré and Hippolyte Lucas was based on Thomas Moore's tale of *Lalla Rookh*, which had also been the story behind Robert Schumann's cantata *Paradise and the Peri* (1843).

Notes

1. This incident was mentioned for the first time by Pigot in 1886. Dean, Cardoze, and Stricker all repeat it in their Bizet biographies without naming their source. Derek Watson, the only Liszt biographer (London, 1984) who mentions the encounter with Bizet ("The tale is told. . . .") in turn quotes Dean.

2. Johann Wolfang von Goethe, *Nationale Dichtkunst*, in *Sämtliche Werke* [Complete works] (Zurich, 1950), 14:557f.

3. Dean, *Bizet* (London, 1975), 49.

CHAPTER EIGHT

Ivan the Terrible and
Leïla, 1863–1865

As far as we know, the *Leïla* libretto is not based on any literary model. For good reason, the title was also soon changed to *Les Pêcheurs de perles* (The Pearl Fishers). There were already plenty of operas named after their heroines. In contrast to Spontini's *La Vestale* and Bellini's *Norma*, the well-known operas that probably guided Carré and Cormon in creating the role of Leïla, in *The Pearl Fishers* the priestess herself sparks, but is not the blaze of the dramatic conflict.

Originally the story's setting was the coast of Mexico. But perhaps because of France's involvement in making Maximilian I the emperor of Mexico, the setting was moved to the Indian Ocean. On 30 September 1863, when the curtain opened at the Théâtre Lyrique to premiere Georges Bizet's first opera, the audience saw the wild coast of an imaginary Ceylon: a few bamboo huts and palm trees, an old Hindu pagoda off in the distance on a cliff over the bright sunlit sea, fishers erecting tents, others drinking and dancing to Indian music. Bizet's music for *The Pearl Fishers'* opening scene is atmospheric and breezy, but headed for the drama to develop. Yet the composer reveals not the slightest intention of including folklore that would suggest orientalism à la Félicien David.

Inhabitants of the southern Indian island make Zurga (baritone) their leader. Nadir (tenor), a hunter who has returned to the island following a long absence, arrives at the beach. He and Zurga reminisce of a woman with whom they were once both in love, but to save their bond she had chosen neither. Zurga and Nadir's duet "Au fond du temple saint" recollects an encounter with her at a Brahman temple. Seizing in this opera the first opportunity to present his music without concession to conventional expectation like focusing the audience's attention or depicting the milieu, Georges Bizet invented a "hit," a highlight of melodic invention, by simply presenting human feelings and relationships. Today every opera fan knows the song, although *The Pearl Fishers* is rarely shown.

Oui, c'est el - le, c'est la dé - es - se plus char - mante__ et plus bel - le,

The *Pearl Fishers* duet was found tacky. In part that was because beginning with the premiere, the unsentimental second half of the duet, "Jurons de resteramis," was truncated. In addition, this little masterpiece of French opera was often ruined by Italian and German pathos fashionable in the twentieth century. More recent French recordings have revealed the work's true simple elegance.

Entering the stage after the duet, the young priestess must promise to remain veiled and chaste in order that her prayers to Brahma, asking him to bless the pearl fishers, will be heard. She is Leïla, the unknown woman. Nadir knows who she is. The audience also senses it because Bizet uses the evocative tune from the duet to remind us. In *Carmen* he later perfected that technique that he used here for the first time.

The chorus "Brahma divin" entirely follows Gounod's model. Offenbach was obviously a model for Leïla and Nadir's romantic duet: despite the ban and despite his oath of friendship to Zurga, Nadir comes to Leïla on the cliff where she prays. Senior priest Nourabad (bass) asks Leïla whether she can keep her promise and she replies that she has done so once before: she had vowed to protect someone on the run and in gratitude that person had given her a necklace and was eventually able to withstand his foes.

The night song, "Comme autrefois," with its considerably Middle-European "horn fifths" creates a severe contrast to the Indian setting. Bizet ignored his audience's longing for something exotic. His music describes circumstances and sentiments as he saw them and in the style that he commanded: in other words, as French. No doubt, his skill at composing would have allowed him to invent songs that his Parisian audience would have taken as being Ceylonese. He does it for a few measures with an oboe solo that reminds us of the oboe solo from his symphony:

When they meet a second time, the lovers are discovered and all but lynched by the betrayed pearl fishers. Zurga intervenes to prevent the worst. He has the priestess unveil her face and when he recognizes Leïla and realizes that Nadir has broken his oath, he wants both killed. Leïla gives the necklace to a fisher that he might give it to her mother, should she die. Zurga recognizes the necklace that had once been his gift to Leïla. A long solo followed by confrontation with her discloses Zurga's character and struggle, effectively employing the evocative melody again, this time dominated by pizzicato syncopation.

Directions for *The Pearl Fishers'* final scene show Nadir seated on a pyre at the foot of a statue of Brahma, drunken Indians dancing frantically, and cups of palm wine being passed around. But Zurga's sense of guilt toward the woman he once loved and who once saved his life is greater than his desire to revenge his vow-breaching friend and his wrath at the unchaste priestess. He sets a fire to divert the attention of the pearl fishers and lets the lovers escape. Everything goes up in flames and alone Zurga remains.

Despite Hector Berlioz's praise in the *Journal des débats*, the work did not meet with broad approval. Carvalho left it on the program for a couple of weeks, alternating it with Mozart's *Figaro*. In the end it was only shown eighteen times during Bizet's lifetime. *The Pearl Fishers* was forgotten until after *Carmen* had worldwide success. In 1893 it was shown again in Paris. By the turn of the century it had almost become part of the standard repertoire, but thereafter it was once again forgotten.

Antoine de Choudens purchased the score to the opera and the performance rights for it, but the original autograph score was lost. Thus we do not know whether what for over a century has come to be known as Bizet's *Pearl Fishers* is authentic or not. For a new showing of it in Paris in 1889 Benjamin Godard made a trio out of a duet, rearranged scenes, and altered the ending: this often-played version ends with Zurga's death. A reliable version was not to be had until Arthur Hammond reconstructed missing score parts using the piano score from 1863 for a production of *The Pearl Fishers* at the Welsh National Opera in Cardiff in 1975. Choudens's handling of Bizet's works at the publishing house he established in 1845 and ran until his death in 1888 has thus often been severely criticized.

At the time *The Pearl Fishers* premiered, Berlioz was rather alone with his favorable opinion of it. Berlioz's judgment was perhaps biased because Carvalho's stage was scheduled to at last produce his own long-completed opera *Les Troyens* (The Trojans). Until then Berlioz had only been able to get fragments performed in Baden-Baden, and in France two years previously his work had been turned down in order to premiere *Tannhäuser*. Even the Théâtre Lyrique had only inadequately rehearsed his *Trojans*. Bizet made an effort to recommend Berlioz's work and his intense intervening on Berlioz's behalf almost led to a duel with Victor Chéri.

Carvalho commissioned Bizet to write a new opera, *Ivan IV*, a story from sixteenth-century Russia. François-Hippolyte Leroy and Henri Trianon had written a libretto for it that in 1855 Charles Gounod had already once considered for the Opéra. Bizet had probably been familiar with the text for some time. Trianon was a man of letters, Leroy was a hands-on man of the stage who worked for various Parisian theaters; among other works, in 1852 he had produced Halévy's *Le Juif errant* (The Wandering Jew) at the Opéra.

Place du Châtelet and the Théâtre Lyrique (on the right), etching by Felix Thorigny

In taking on the music for *Ivan IV*, Bizet tried out the larger format required by "historical" narrative.

Meanwhile, Adolphe and Georges Bizet, Marie Reiter, and her son Jean all lived on rue Fontaine (in today's ninth arrondissement). Shortly after the premiering of *The Pearl Fishers*, Adolphe had bought property in Le Vésinet outside of town on the Seine and had two summer homes built on it.

In March 1864 Bizet viewed the premiere of Gounod's *Mireille*, whose musical idiom went well with the work's—partly authentic—folklore elements. The end of the month brought the unveiling of a Halévy monument. A severe nervous disorder kept Bizet's teacher's widow from the ceremony.

Fifteen-year-old Geneviève Halévy left home because her mother held her responsible for the death of her sister Esther. Esther Halévy, who was thought engaged to their cousin Ludovic, died under admittedly peculiar circumstances, but it was probably a natural death accompanied by a nervous disorder. Bizet had remained in close contact to the family. But he had not started finishing Halévy's opera *Noé*. That spring he was working on *Ivan IV* and helping Hector Berlioz with rehearsals for *L'Enfance du Christ* (The Childhood of Christ).

In May 1864, Giacomo Meyerbeer died. Bizet attended the pompous obsequies; the German composer's remains were returned to Berlin.

At the Théâtre Lyrique, Bizet's *Ivan IV* was scheduled to follow *Mireille*. The latter included a melody for a Provençal shepherd song that had initially been intended for the young Bulgarian in Gounod's own version of *Ivan IV*. Folklore, in other words, was completely interchangeable. But Gounod had struggled with the libretto for *Ivan* that had neither a toehold for conventional genre tableaus, nor true lovers in the plot. Trianon and Leroy, perhaps following Nikolai M. Karamsin's portrayal of Russian history, had written a libretto in Scribe-Meyerbeer style, however, it lacked Scribe and Meyerbeer's specific sense of stylistic integrity, historical plausibility, and particularly, effectiveness on the stage. Their *Ivan IV* had its obvious dramatic moments, but no vital figures to create relationships full of suspense.

A Cherkessk princess named Marie is abducted and brought to the tsar's court after helping a young Bulgarian and his master who had lost their way through the mountains. The unnamed master was in reality Tsar Ivan in disguise, who now recognizes Marie when she is presented as a prisoner of the court. He desires to marry her, but she consents only under coercion. This angers a certain Yorloff, who wanted to marry off his own daughter to the tsar. He approaches King Temrouk and his son Igor, the prince of Cherkessk, who have set off for Moscow to rescue Maria. Yorloff schemes to compromise the young tsarina by getting her brother into her chamber and then letting Ivan accidentally discover them together. The plan works, and when the tsar also finds out that Temrouk has set the Kremlin on fire, he is shocked. Yorloff tries to usurp the throne and have the Cherkessk siblings executed. But Ivan recollects his wits and Yorloff dies on the scaffold. The story ends with a hymn to divine justice.

Through the music, and with some skill, Bizet tried to make this abstruse story pliable for the stage. The first act's charming depiction of girls drawing water in a Caucasian idyll makes no effort to be exotically folkloristic; on the contrary, the scene ends with sounds that remind us of *Lohengrin*. The brass parts clearly remind us of Wagner's prelude to act 3 of *Lohengrin* and the string melodies underlying the Cherkessk princess's appearance as a Kremlin prisoner are reminiscent of Wagner's grail motifs. The song sung by the young Bulgarian is nothing other than the soprano bolero sung by the Portuguese officer in *Vasco da Gama*!

Bizet had given up hope that his envoi cantata *Vasco da Gama* would ever be performed because in April 1865 Meyerbeer's opera *L'Africaine* (The African Woman) had been premiered posthumously with the figure of Vasco da Gama as the main male role.

When it came to effects, Bizet approached act 2 of *Ivan IV* with equal nonchalance: Ivan's sister Olga sings along with a group of nuns to the sound of an imaginary Kremlin organ! Ivan's simple music-hall war song, his sole aria in a five-act opera of which he is the leading hero, reminds us of the gaudy syncopation in Verdi's *Trovatore* gypsy choir. The act also ends sounding very much like Verdi. The *chœur dansé* for the wedding scene in act 3 is clearly modeled after Gounod. The conspiracy duet by the father and son reminds us of *The Masked Ball*. Then we hear music for a procession and sounds from the organ that remind us of the dramaturgical arrangement for act 2 of *Lohengrin*. "Venez souveraine adore," the aria for the young Bulgarian that opens act 4, was taken directly from the cantata *Le Golfe de Baïa* that Bizet wrote as a piano score in 1856, the first time he competed for the Prix de Rome. But despite all this eclecticism, Bizet did manage to include some original passages. Igor's aria "Pourquoi revenez vous" sounds like a draft for Don José in *Carmen*. But the only moment in *Ivan IV* where Bizet really successfully exploits his own skill at condensed dramatic exposition and atmospheric development is the introduction to act 5.

We hear this melody in a scene where an officer uses a password to get through the wall surrounding the Kremlin. Rumors spread that the tsar was dead. Here the combination of secretive apprehension on the one hand and temerity on the other already displays something of the smuggler scene from act 3 of *Carmen*.

Bizet composed most of the music for *Ivan IV* at Le Vésinet and pressed for time because to earn a living he had to work on other compositions and give lessons as well. In the autumn of 1865 copies of the material were made for staging *Ivan*, but then Carvalho ran out of money. In December Bizet wrote to Edmond Galabert, whom he instructed in composition by letter, that the production of *Ivan IV* had been postponed and that ultimately he had withdrawn the work from the Théâtre Lyrique.

He tried in vain to offer the piece to the Opéra. He was also particularly peeved that after having dropped *Ivan IV* for financial reasons, on 30 December 1865 the Théâtre Lyrique nonetheless premiered *La Fiancée d'Abydos*, an opera by Adrien Barthe, who had won the Rodrigues Award in 1858 for his *Te Deum*. Early biographers reported that Bizet then burned his score for *Ivan IV*. But based on information from Émile Vuillermoz, Maurice Tassart and other authors believed that Bizet kept the score to wait for a better opportunity to have the work performed.[1] Speculation that the premiere of *Ivan IV* was canceled out of political consideration for Moscow's tsar, who planned to visit Paris, are unproven.[2] It is possible that Bizet destroyed the copy of the manuscript that he had offered to the Opéra, but in 1929 Bizet's widow's second husband gave a different copy to the archive of the Conservatoire. The fifth act of that score is not fully instrumented, thus it can hardly be the version that Bizet offered to the Opéra. In any case, Bizet felt that his "Ceylonese" opera had brought him further than the tsar drama and he let the latter very deliberately disappear into a drawer, as we can see from the fact that he used parts of it in other contexts.

During World War II the score for Bizet's *Ivan* that until then had never been performed was said to have been microfilmed by German occupiers in order to prepare a revised version of the work for performance in Dresden.[3] In 1933 Chantavoine had reported that the score exists, and in 1938 it had been displayed at an exhibition honoring Bizet's one hundredth birthday. But due to the war, the production in Dresden never happened. The alleged German "rediscoverer"[4] of *Ivan IV*, Ernst Hartmann (who became a secondary school teacher in Horb am Neckar after 1945), is said to have completed the instrumentation for act 5. As Winton Dean reports, in Paris Hartmann apparently also organized a private performance of the work with piano accompaniment while the city was still occupied. Winton Dean, the latest edition of a German encyclopedia for music (*Musik in Geschichte und Gegen-wart*), and Hervé Lacombe (in his French Bizet biography published in 2000) all continue to claim that *Ivan IV* was "premiered" in 1946 at the "Castle of Mühringen."[5] But there, under circumstances of reversed occupation, only some excerpts of the work were shown to a private audience and accompanied only by a piano.[6] They changed the title to *Yvan le terrible* (Ivan the Terrible), although—according to Mina Curtiss—song texts were unaltered.

To commemorate the centenary of Bizet's death, on 3 October 1975 at a concert by the BBC Northern Orchestra conducted by Bryden Thomson in Manchester the music from *Ivan IV* was performed for the first time as (to the best of our knowledge) the composer had indicated it should be. Based on the preserved manuscript, Howard Williams had written an unabridged version of the opera, adding what was needed to make it performable. A different production that included the scenes had already once been shown in 1951 at the Grand Théâtre in Bordeaux based on a version written by Henri Busser for Editions Choudens. Busser, who sometimes signed his name "Büsser" (his German family name), had studied under Gounod and Guiraud and in 1893 had won the Prix de Rome. He filled in the missing instrument parts, but also omitted some passages from the score and made four acts out of five. He also turned the indisputably trousers role (a male character sung by a woman) of the young Bulgarian into a role for a tenor, considerably distorting the

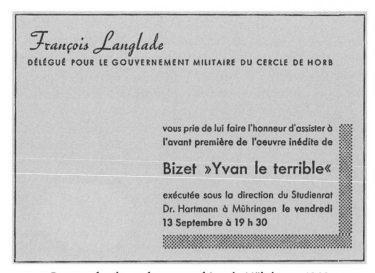

Program for the performance of *Ivan* in Mühringen, 1946

impression one gets of Bizet's music. His version was also used for the first German public premiere of the opera in 1951 in Cologne.[7] In 2002 Radio France broadcasted a concert performance of the version by Williams, which has been recorded on a CD.

Notes

1. Accompanying text for the record with excerpts from *Ivan IV* (Pathé Marconi 2908631) as conducted by Georges Tzipine, 1957.

2. Henri Busser also claims this in the foreword to his edition of *Ivan*. He also says that the Théâtre Lyrique immediately played *La Jolie fille de Perth* instead of *Ivan IV*. The latter claim is definitely wrong, and the first claim very probably does not match the facts.

3. Titled *König Turpin* (King Turpin) and relocated to take place at the Merovingian court of the sixth century.

4. Hans J. Moser, *Musikgeschichte in 100 Lebensbildern* (Stuttgart, 1958), 756.

5. Schloss Hohenmühringen, a privately owned castle in the Mühringen quarter of the town of Horb am Neckar. The commissioner of the French military government for the county of Horb, Françoise Langlade, had issued invitations to this performance.

6. As stated by Claire Luz-Fassbender, who sang the arias for both the young Bulgarian and for Marie.

7. Translated by Fritz Schröder, the work was presented as *Iwan* at the Cologne Opera's makeshift stage in the auditorium of the university during the playing season of 1951–1952 under the musical direction of Richard Kraus with Anny Schlemm singing the part of Marie.

CHAPTER NINE

Arrangements and Rhine Romanticism, 1865–1866

With no money coming in from his latest opera, Bizet took on odd jobs for various publishers, not only for Choudens, but for Heugel and Hartmann as well. He was used to working fast and it was relatively easy for him to write piano arrangements for currently running operas like Mozart's *Don Giovanni* within a very short time. *Don Giovanni*, starring Christine Nilsson as Donna Elvira and Adelina Patti as Zerlina, was a huge success at the Théâtre Lyrique just then.

During that era piano arrangements made from opera scores were not piano scores as we know them today that enable one to play the orchestra part on a keyboard instrument. Piano scores during Bizet's times also included solo and choir parts. The purpose of these transcriptions was to allow opera fans to later relive their evening at the theater at home. Bizet wrote piano versions for individual numbers from operas by Ambroise Thomas, and he worked out a collection of popular opera choruses by Gounod. For Heugel he elaborated a large collection of opera arrangements titled *Le Pianiste chanteur* containing two series each of excerpts from French, Italian, and German operas. There was also a great demand for four-handed piano arrangements; Bizet wrote them for "Casta Diva" from Bellini's *Norma*, and for *Méditation de Ch. Gounod sur le premier prelude de Bach*, better known as *Ave Maria* by Bach/Gounod. Salon orchestra adaptations for chamber music at home were also a steady source of income. These less creative minor tasks, however, helped improve Bizet's technical skill for working on his own scores.

Because he had meanwhile made a profitable name for himself with *The Pearl Fishers*, it made good business sense to furnish the market with a few popular compositions of his own. *Gebrauchsmusik* was in demand: piano pieces of light to intermediate levels of difficulty and songs with piano accompaniment. Bizet's *La Chasse fantastique* (The Fantastic Hunt) was a hit. Marmontel, to whom it is dedicated, liked it, too: "It has the knightly and diabolic sound of old legends. It's an imaginative work . . . an epic ride through the unseen."[1] It has often been suggested that Bizet's music reflecting the hunt might have been a piano version of the lost symphonic overture *La Chasse d'Ossian*, but that is unlikely: with its resounding arpeggios the work is very clearly intended for salon virtuosity. Bizet did not have an orchestra in mind here. The slow first measures remind us of Weber's rondo *Aufforderung zum Tanz* (Asking for a Dance). The most characteristic trait of the piece is its amusing play on hunting horn motifs.

At the time, the most important instance of fashionable French Rhine romanticism was Victor Hugo's *Le Rhin: Lettres à un ami* from 1842. Hugo, who lived on the island of Guernsey, had made sketches during his trip down the Rhine. French readers had such a thirst for poetic descriptions and tales inspired by the major river on their country's eastern border that many authors scrambled to satisfy them, with varying results. Among them was Joseph Méry (1798–1865) who in 1858 published his comprehensive work called *Ems et le bords du Rhin*. Today we remember Méry especially for cooperating on the libretto for Verdi's *Don Carlos*, but Bizet knew him from the premiere of *Érostrate* in Baden-Baden because Méry had written that libretto for Reyer. Reyer, too, had put music to *L'Hymne du Rhin*, one of Méry's texts for solos, choir, and an orchestra.

Ever since the appearance of Madame de Staël's book *L'Allemagne* in 1813, the Rhine with its castles, vineyards, and tributary valleys nesting spa resorts adored by the French (such as Ems, Baden-Baden, and Bad Schwalbach where the empress Eugénie took the waters) had become a motif in French literature. Composers were naturally also affected by that trend, but by 1865 purely literary enthusiasm for the Rhine had passed its zenith and begun to take on political undertones.

Nonetheless, publisher Heugel asked Bizet to write something along those lines, though in a smaller format: Méry's standard Rhine poetry provided the template for Bizet's *Chants du Rhin* (Melodies of the Rhine), characterized by a romantic manner and imaginative rhapsodic descriptions of places not too remote and yet somehow foreign. In *Prélude*, the first of his *Rhinegesänge* (Rhine Songs), Méry suggests that not only Beethoven, but Gluck, Mozart, and Weber, too, all came from the "blue bays" of the Rhine River.[2] His

Le Pianiste chanteur. **Cover page of piano arrangements by Bizet.** *Conservatoire National de Musique, Paris*

impressions of the Rhine even included a gypsy woman, celebrated in the fourth, scherzo-like piece of the song cycle called *La Bohèmienne*. Bizet gave it a rather Hungarian sound reminiscent of Liszt.

The most conspicuously programmatic parts are the second and the last of the *Chants du Rhin* where clip-clopping hooves and intense allure depict departure and return. *Le Retour* is dedicated to Camille Saint-Saëns. But overall the work is marked by a rather noncommittal and uniform feeling that was common for the "songs without words" so fashionable at the time. In *Confidences* Bizet did not make even the slightest attempt to find some musical association with the title as, for example, Robert Schumann had done for *Wichtige Begebenheit* (An Important Event).[3] Nonetheless, Bizet's *Chants du Rhin* sold well and later Maurice le Boucher, winner of the Prix de Rome in 1907, even adapted them for the orchestra.

Michel Cardoze's Bizet biography dedicates an entire chapter to an encounter that happened in the autumn of 1865. A woman of enigmatic repute had become Bizet's neighbor in Le Vésinet. The meanwhile twenty-seven-year-old composer met her on a local train. Born as Elisabeth Céleste Vénard, the forty-year-old woman now went by the name of Céleste Mogador. She had been a circus rider and actress and the mistress of numerous influential men, including artist Alfred de Musset. She is said to have taken money for her company, such that Winton Dean explicitly calls her a whore. Before her stage career as a dancer she had actually worked in that milieu. She married the French consul Count Moreton de Chabrillan and moved to Australia, but four years before he died in 1858 she returned to France. She wrote stories and pieces for the stage, although her knowledge of literary French was limited. Her books sold well anyway. For a short while in 1865 she tried to become the principal female actress at the Théâtre Marigny on Champs-Élysées, where Offenbach had once played.

After her death in 1909 a sequel was found to the memoirs she had already published during her lifetime that told of the young composer whose summer house was close to her own Chalet Lionel (the first name of her deceased husband, the count). But certainly these late reminiscences of a very old demimondaine can hardly serve as a reliable source of information on Bizet, who by that time had been long dead and world famous.

Surely they would have had a good neighborly relationship, especially being both artists, although of quite different kinds. It is said that sometimes Céleste Mogador sang little songs by Sebastián Yradier (1809–1865) at cafés. The Basque Yradier had come to Paris as the singing teacher for Empress Eugénie from Spain and had become a fairly popular salon composer. Even Adelina Patti and Pauline Viardot sang songs by Yradier, and both Georges and Adolphe Bizet owned some of his pieces. The fact that Georges Bizet later borrowed an Yradier melody for *Carmen* was probably fortuitous and circumstantial, just like Mogador's performances of "Ay Chiquita." Later some tried to see some significant connection between Mogador and *Carmen*, as if Céleste had been a model for the opera figure. But Yradier's most famous melody, more well known than even Bizet's havanaise based on Yradier's song "El Arreglito," is and remains "La Paloma"!

"Was Céleste important? Oh oui!" says Cardoze. But for Georges Bizet she was, on the outskirts of town, probably no more and no less than an entertaining diversion from his busy workdays. Her house was larger than his and she had a grand piano in her salon, where he occasionally liked to play.

Bizet's *Chants du Rhin* were published in early 1866; Joseph Méry died in June of the same year. Bizet occasionally gave a piano concert, usually playing his own works and arrangements, not to make himself a name as a concert pianist, but instead to be appreciated as a piano-playing composer. Gounod had introduced him to Princess Mathilde, the daughter of Jérôme, Napoleon I's youngest brother who had died in 1860. The princess asked him occasionally to play at social events. He continued to work on songs; another order for an opera was nowhere in sight.

Céleste Mogador. *Bibliothèque Nationale, Paris*

This kind of song, called a *mélodie* in French (sometimes also called a *lied*, when it followed German models), was very popular. Most of these songs, even by renowned composers, were—like Bizet's own—individual pieces written for music making at home. One great exception—even during the composer's lifetime—were the six lieder written by Hector Berlioz in 1834 based on poems by Théophile Gautier, a collection titled *Les Nuits d'été* (Summer Nights).

Bizet had already once composed a melody for a text by Victor Hugo, the patriarch of French literature, but had not yet had it published: *Les Adieux de l'hôtesse arabe* from the collection of poems called *Les Orientales*. Winton Dean admired it.[4]

Above an ostinato rhythm, Bizet develops a melancholy cantilena in which a yearning oriental beauty says adieu to a "jeun'homme—beau voyageur" who is moving on.

The piece ends with coloraturas similar to those in Verdi's Moorish song for Princess Eboli, the *Chanson du voile* from *Don Carlos*. As in *Pastorale*, a lied that he wrote in 1868 based on an ostinato Sicilian rhythm, here we already see voice treatment suggestive of the figure of Carmen and two of the figures that preceded her, Mab and Djamileh. Bizet definitely followed the oriental style cast by Félicien David that, while it did not present the Orient authentically,[5] did accurately mirror the text's equally inauthentic exoticism.

In 1866 Heugel printed six songs by Bizet collected as *Feuilles d'album* (Album Pages). The words were, among others, by Victor Hugo, and by Alphonse de Lamartine, whose poem *L'Âme triste est pareille au doux ciel* had once been Bizet's very first attempt at working with a *mélodie*. (As a young man Richard Wagner, too, had put music to verse by Victor Hugo and by Pierre de Ronsard, whose *Sonnet* is also among Bizet's "Album Pages.")[6] Bizet's music for Hugo's *Guitare* presents a spirited rhythmic anticipation of dance moments from *Carmen*.

Adieux à Suzon, music for a poem by Alfred de Musset, is one of Bizet's few longer single *mélodie* compositions. Here Bizet clearly broke with conventional expectations for a *mélodie* because the text perceptibly requires more than a one-dimensional sentiment. Despite his routine grasp, Bizet's brilliant treatment of the text and voice, his deliberate use of melisma, and an effective piano part can be seen very clearly in *Chanson d'avril* (April Song, based on a text by Louis Bouilhet) where he skillfully makes the cry "l'amour" the focus and epitome of attention.

But two other *mélodies* by Bizet are difficult to rank among the miscellaneous texts that he put to music: *La Chanson du fou* based on a text by Hugo that he probably composed in 1868, and *Absence*, published in 1872, whose origin we cannot date. The *Chanson du fou* is declamatory and monotonous in both rhythm and melody. Its introverted melancholy and simple, but pointed piano accompaniment are reminiscent of Schubert's *Winterreise* (Winter Journey).

Here Bizet let himself be moved by the strong text, making no recognizable concessions to popular taste. Significantly, it is the only lied by Bizet that Dietrich Fischer-Dieskau recorded.[7]

It was certainly not a coincidence that Bizet one day wrote music for Théophile Gautier's poem *Absence*. In 1834 Berlioz had already included the first three of the eight verses of *Absence* in *Les Nuits d'été*. Bizet dropped the third verse and let the sixth and eighth follow Gautier's verse one and two, fully exploiting the poetic picture that is only alluded to in the passages that Berlioz had used: "Go there, my heart, for me, and light like a wounded dove on the edge of her roof." In contrast to Berlioz, Bizet followed the intentions of the poet without subjecting them to a personal desire for self-expression. He found an adequate two-part musical form for four of Gautier's verses without changing the style of the poetry.

It was not Bizet's habit to penetrate words with music, or even make up his own musical language, as Wagner had done for musical drama. For Bizet the stage, the plot, and the nature of people and places produced the organic cohesion between words and music, allowing each to maintain its integrity. As a composer of lieder he thus barely went beyond what was fashionable.

He sometimes thought of doing an independent opera project and occasionally outlined some themes, but these sketches were never very detailed because he was realistic. It was pointless to waste time on projects with uncertain prospects of ever being performed. Instead, he waited for one of Paris's three opera stages to approach him: that was how to get better libretti. Many of the lieder that were published posthumously by Choudens and by Bizet's heirs were simply passages taken from his musical sketches, to which they added texts; these pieces are not authentic.

Meanwhile Léon Carvalho had improved the Théâtre Lyrique's finances sufficiently to be able to propose a new opera schedule to Bizet. Under Carvalho's direction, Paris's Théâtre Lyrique came third after the Opéra and the Opéra Comique in promoting innovative French opera. By then Carvalho had already directed it for ten years, actively supported by his wife, singer Caroline Miolan, who had studied under Bizet's uncle Delsarte. Born in 1825 on Mauritius as Léon Carvaille, Carvalho had not only sharpened the profile of the Théâtre Lyrique by staging important premieres, he also made it the site of the French premieres of many works by Mozart, as well as of pieces by Verdi and Wagner produced in French.

Bizet signed an agreement with Carvalho in July 1866. Earlier that month Prussian troops under Bismarck and Moltke had defeated the Austrian army near Königgrätz in Bohemia, weakening Napoleon III's interest in Italy. The Kingdom of Italy, which now included Venetia, could now more easily stand up to the Papal State in Rome that got support from France. In France there was a cry for "revenge for Sadowa" (the French name for Königgrätz). The French emperor claimed regions west of the Rhine, including Mainz and Luxembourg.

Notes

1. Taken from remarks made by Michel Poupet in the accompanying text for the recording of the complete piano works by Bizet (*Le Chant du monde*, LDC 278.776/7).

2. "Dans se golfes d'azur, où les aigles vont boire, / dans les nefs de ses bois, divin conservatoire, / il créa Glück, Weber, Beethoven et Mozart." J. Méry, *Chants du Rhin*, taken from M. Muller, *L'Œuvre pianistique originale de Georges Bizet* (Yverdon, 1976), 96.

3. No. 6 from *Kinderszenen* [Scenes from childhood], op. 15.

4. Dean, *Bizet* (London, 1975), 63.

5. Peter Gradenwitz, "Félicien David and French Romantic Orientalism," *Musical Quarterly* 62 (1976):502.

6. Richard Wagner, *Trois mélodies* (Paris, 1839). Pierre de Ronsard (1525–1585) was a French poet of the Renaissance whose work was modeled on Petrarch.

7. *Mélodies de la Belle Époque*, Teldec 8.43754 ZK.

CHAPTER TEN

A Gypsy in Scotland, 1866–1868

The Opéra Comique announced that in November 1866 it would premiere Ambroise Thomas's *Mignon*. The libretto for the opera based on Goethe's *Wilhelm Meister* had been written by Barbier and Carré, who had already once adapted Goethe's *Faust* for the French stage for Gounod. The story took place in Germany and Italy, but gypsy dances and choruses gave even *Mignon* a folklore touch. Carvalho decided not to use straightforwardly oriental material. He commissioned authors Jules-Henri Vernoy de Saint-Georges and Jules Adenis, both experienced but not top-notch authors, to write a libretto for Walter Scott's *St. Valentine's Day, or the Fair Maid of Perth*. Vernoy de Saint-Georges was the more important of the two. For many years he had directed the Opéra Comique and, having worked in the field for forty years, he had also collaborated with Scribe for Auber, written a *Falstaff* libretto for Adolphe Adam, done five librettos for Flotow, and also written the text for Clapisson's *Fanchonette*.

In the early nineteenth century, Sir Walter Scott's (1771–1832) historical novels were popular throughout Europe. The history and legends of Scotland's knights and castles, its romantic scenery, lovely mysterious women, and both real and imaginary picturesque figures provided a romantic backdrop and fascinating plots for Scott's books and their stories came to be used in many an opera. As early as 1826, Antonio Pacini had written a pasticcio for Scott's *Ivanhoe*, using music from various works by Rossini. Later Otto Nicolai used the same story for the opera *Templario*. There were also opera versions of Scott's *Kenilworth* and *Lady of the Lake*.[1] But during Bizet's lifetime the most famous opera based on a story by Scott was not—as it is today—Donizetti's *Lucia* based on *The Bride of Lammermoor*, but Boieldieu's *La Dame blanche* (The White Lady), for which Scribe had used a variety of Scott's motifs.

St. Valentine's Day plays in the city of Perth, the seat of Scottish kings in the early fifteenth century. "While the book does lack careful attention to the typical Scottish ambiance so characteristic of the author's other Scotland novels, on the other hand it has the advantage that its fictitious plot and historical realism complement and significantly augment one another. Although Scott assembles an arsenal of romantic props for the plot, his depiction of the feudal system of the late Middle Ages, falling apart because of power struggles among the privileged and a disregard for human dignity, is thoroughly anti-romantic," writes Jérôme von Gebsattel.[2] Oddly, in those days in France the epitome of romanticism in the theater was thought to be works by Shakespeare and Goethe, although not the musical adaptations of their dramas. In Germany, in contrast, the two were seen as representative of the classical era in literature. In French opera, however, the *drame lyrique* works by Gounod and later also Bizet, led to verism. The era of explicit romanticism in German opera, as exemplified by *Freischütz* (The Marksman, 1821) and *Parsifal*, had no counterpart in France.

Even the literary idea behind *La Jolie fille de Perth*, then, suggests nothing like any kind of opera-adequate bagpipe music. To give it the right touch, the librettists simply turned the Provençal (!) ballad monger Louise into the obligatory female opera gypsy, giving her—strangely enough—the name "Mab" from an old Irish legendary figure. Carvalho may have requested this dramaturgical label fraud. Gounod's version of *Romeo and Juliet*, namely, was scheduled for showing prior to Bizet's opera. In Shakespeare's *Romeo and Juliet* Mercutio's mention of Queen Mab, "the fairies' midwife of dreams," is rather marginal; in Gounod's opera, however, the *Ballade de la Reine Mab*, she is the musical focus of the entire first act. Parisians were also familiar with the scherzo *La Reine Mab* from Berlioz's symphony *Romeo et Juliette*.

The practical concessions that had to be made for the stage and the sustained impact that such compromises had on the reception of Bizet's second opera for Carvalho began right with the premiere. Having completed the score in record time, Bizet was then forced to omit passages. Subsequent publishers and editors mangled it even more. In 1985, finally, a fairly authentic original version was reconstructed by David Lloyd Jones based on Bizet's papers and became the first and now only recording of the piece.[3]

Max Kalbeck, whose judgment was highly respected and instructive, though not always fair, and in the case of *The Fair Maid*—since he had no knowledge of the original score—had no way of being fair, said after its premiere in Vienna in 1883 based on an adaptation by Julius Hopp: "It sounds like Auber and Gounod, and Beethoven, Weber, Schubert, and Marschner, with a tint of Wagner, Verdi, Meyerbeer, and Offenbach . . . in other words in somewhat mottled, but overall good and distinguished company. Only one composer . . . is hardly recognizable, namely, Bizet himself. . . . As weak as Bizet's music is, trying as it does to do justice to the libretto, we have to admire the composer for being able to make this nonsense work on the stage at all."[4] Eventually Kalbeck published his own adaptation of Bizet's opera "for the German stage," which was even further removed from the original.

When Bizet finally got the libretto that had been completed at the last minute and could start writing music for it, he wrote to Edmond Galabert: "My *Maid of Perth* has little similarity to the novel. It is a dramatic piece, but the figures lack character. I hope to solve the problem. There are some verses for which I simply cannot set the words to music; not a single note comes to mind."[5]

Act 1 opens in tenor Henry Smith's weaponry workshop. One after another a few awaited and a few unexpected guests drop by. First comes Mab, seeking safety from some importunate men. Then Glover (a maker of gloves) comes in with his daughter Catherine, to whom Smith—on this Valentine's Day—would like to become engaged, along with Glover's apprentice Ralph. Glover brings some "pâté, old Scotch whiskey, and succulent pudding," creating one of the libretto's few clues as to where the story happens. An unknown man enters the workshop to have his dagger repaired; later Glover will recognize him as the prince and Duke of Rothsay. The duke, a Martin-baritone,[6] harasses Catherine, and Smith becomes violent. (In Scott's novel, Rothsay breaks into Glover's home to kidnap Catherine, but Smith thwarts his attempt.) Mab comes out from her hiding place in order to protect the duke, with whom she is having an affair. Catherine thinks that the gypsy woman is her rival for Smith's love. Everyone is confused but enjoys the pâté, pudding, and whiskey. Bizet fills the scene with a very atmospheric orchestra prelude that contains two of his typically lyrical melodies.

Glover's drinking song is a sterling couplet of a rather conventional kind. Technically, the same is true of Mab's couplet, but not for the song's overall treatment of vocal expression. Here we find considerable premonition of Carmen's role. It is not quite clear what voice should sing this role. Stereotypically, opera gypsies were expected to be alto singers, or at least mezzo-soprano, as they were in Verdi's *Troubadour*, *Masked Ball*, and *Force of Destiny*, and in Gounod's *Mireille*. But Mab is basically a soprano role, at most a light coloratura mezzo-soprano of the kind we find in Rossini. Mab's difficult couplet "Catherine est coquette" was probably omitted for the first showing.

Catherine's aria "Vive l'hiver," where she sings of the carnival, is the only time in an opera that Bizet fulfills the wishes of a virtuoso prima donna, for whom other composers were much more willing to make concessions. Carvalho had originally intended to have prominent Christine Nilsson play the role of the fair maid. Having her name on the program would have lessened the financial risk of premiering the piece.[7] But ultimately Jane Devriès sang the part instead.

In a trio for Catherine, Smith, and the incognito duke, Bizet finds a new tone that turns up again in the quintet in *Carmen* ("De ce beau seigneur l'insolence . . ."). But Bizet could come up with nothing for one of the weakest spots in Saint-Georges and Adenis's text, the quartet that includes Catherine and Mab (who until then had been hiding): "Ah! La rencontre est imprévue! Une femme? Ah! Le séducteur!—Oui, sa présence inattendue a desarmé mon bras vengeur!" (Alas! The encounter was unforeseen! A woman? Alas! The seducer!—Yes, his unexpected appearance has rendered my vengeful arms helpless!) In the novel the fair maid Catherine lures the duke, who is madly in love with her, to a remote castle where he dies. In the opera libretto the anemic duke lives on.

Act 2 begins with citizens on night watch marching and singing at Perth's main square. Here, once again, as he did for the first scene in *Don Procopio* and the last act of *Ivan IV*, Bizet demonstrates his talent for creating a stage full of atmosphere.

Bons ci - to-yens, bons ci - to-yens, dor - mez! Tout est calme et tran - quil - le,

The scene is followed by Mab's companions torch dancing through the Scottish city, an episode that was later often used in *Carmen* ballet. Hugo Wolf, normally reserved at praising other musicians, found *Jolie fille* "absolutely delightful, a wildly graceful piece of music," with its "titillating rhythms and odd harmonies."[8] Later the dance was thrown together with an orchestra version of *Chœur de la ronde de nuit* (not arranged by Bizet), the prelude to *Jolie fille*, and Smith's serenade, and became a popular suite with the ridiculous name of *Gypsy Scenes*, while the opera *La Jolie fille de Perth* paled increasingly in comparison to *Carmen*.

Bizet had agreed to deliver the score for *Jolie fille* in December 1866. He interrupted the work only to finish a small piece that had been commissioned for a Belgian men's choir that was based on a text by Hugo. Called *Saint Jean de Pathmos*, it is the only a cappella music that Bizet wrote. He then met Carvalho's deadline for *Jolie fille*, but only by making use of parts from the unpublished score for *Don Procopio*. We detect it first in the carnival chorus:

He then used the notes from Don Odoardo's serenade for Smith's serenade with the text "À la voix d'un amant fidèle." But to this exercise in style from his days in Italy and his first opera he then added proof of how his own sense of melody had meanwhile matured:

Having sung below Catherine's balcony in vain, Smith surmises that his damsel must be at the castle of the lusty duke. Apprentice Ralph, a weak version of Scott's much more sophisticated figure Conachar (another of Catherine's suitors), ultimately has a long solo in a potpourri of styles (Caspar from *Freischütz*, Omin from *Abduction*, and Marcel from *The Huguenots*); it was an attempt to produce the old cliché of the bass singer who takes comfort from the bottle.

Act 3 centers on the duke's cavatina "Elle sortait de sa demeure," a sophisticated bravura often omitted from printed piano scores for *La Jolie fille de Perth*. At Rothsay's castle, Smith searches for Catherine in vain. Finally she arrives along with her father who has come to invite the duke to his daughter's wedding to Smith. Smith discovers a rose he had given to Catherine, now pinned to the duke's clothing. But the latter had gotten it from jealous Mab, after Catherine, in act 1, had thrown it to the floor. Smith accuses

Catherine of betraying him. Catherine loses her mind, giving the piece a reason for a scene of delirium, like those in Donizetti's *Lucia di Lammermoor* and Meyerbeer's *L'Étoile du Nord*, which was probably Saint-Georges and Adenis's intention in crisscrossing the plot.

Ralph tries to persuade Smith to be fair; a duel between the two is planned to eliminate doubt over Catherine's virtue. Scott's story tells of a bloody battle between Conachar's clan and an enemy, at the end of which Conachar stands alone against his archfiend Smith and commits suicide, so that Catherine can marry Smith. The opera, in contrast, celebrates St. Valentine's, and when Mab discovers that befuddled Catherine does not understand the news that the duke prevented the duel and that Smith is not dead, she uses a psychotherapeutic trick: she dresses as Catherine and repeats the scene from act 2 where Smith sang his serenade for Catherine in vain. The fair maid from Perth returns to her senses, and the opera ends on a reconciliatory note.

On 29 December 1866, Carvalho received the score completed in a rush for *Jolie fille*. But for various reasons the final dress rehearsal did not happen until September 1867. Its showing was in part postponed because in the meantime Liverpool-born Adolphe Devin-Duvivier had premiered his opera *Deborah* based on Scott's tale of Ivanhoe. It helped, of course, that Devin-Duvivier paid the production costs out of his own pocket. And just three weeks after that performance, the Théâtre Lyrique staged another novelty: *Sardanapale*, an opera based on Byron by Wagnerian Félix-Ludger Rossignol, who also went by the name of Victorin de Joncières.

That winter Parisians also enjoyed a new entertaining period play with music by Jacques Offenbach that was showing at the theater of the royal palace: *La Vie parisienne*, a work by Ludovic Halévy and Henri Meilhac that cleverly mocked life in Paris under Napoleon III. Georges Bizet, now twenty-eight years old, would probably have gone to a performance of the "pièce en 5 actes mêlée de chant" to enjoy the skillfully written dialogues and carefully composed songs with Offenbach's elegant music as a welcome diversion from his travail with the Scottish opera nonsense.

Bizet knew that he had done his best with the score, but his own understanding of the musical theater was too holistic to make up for all of the libretto's flaws. He was tired of seeing opera keep recycling the old characters and plots as interchangeable excuses for listening to beautiful music.

Meilhac and Halévy had already written successful comedies together as well as the libretto for Offenbach's opera *Barbe Bleue* (Bluebeard), staged in the spring of 1866. Now they were collaborating on another text for Offenbach. They took motifs from Eugène Sue's *Mystères de Paris* (The Mysteries of Paris) to write the libretto for *La Grande-Duchess de Gérolstein* (The Grand Duchess of Gerolstein). Halévy and Meilhac were masters at converting better literary texts into audience favorites that were nonetheless worthy texts for the musical theater.

Regarding Meilhac's work with Offenbach, Eduard Hanslick writes: "In France authors and composers always work together to create an opera. . . . [In Germany] the author and the composer often never meet. . . . There the composer is nailed to the libretto like a board, the French composer sees the libretto as a living creature that unfolds in his hands."[9] Unfortunately, in this case the famous music critic Hanslick made a generalization that in reality was a fortunate exception.

The success of Offenbach's operas buffas marked the definitive end of opera comique as an independent form of buoyant musical theater. The Bouffes-Parisiens offered brilliant entertainment with "light" music without the increasingly growing extravagance demanded by opera comique. Offenbach, as Siegfried Kracauer has said, led an "attack on pomp."[10] For Offenbach the pared-down instrumentation that gave his scores their own charm had long since become not merely a limitation born of necessity, but a principle of opposition. Simple melodies made his theater more direct. Georges Bizet followed developments in Offenbach attentively; after all, it had been Offenbach who through his *Doctor Miracle* contest had helped him realize that he could do more than work in the humorous genre alone. Bizet shared Offenbach's respect for "details that oppose bloated ostentatiousness."[11] Eventually, with *Carmen* he made the lack of superficial display associated with the grand opera exemplarily serve the plot.

In 1867, another world exhibition again shaped the musical and theatrical life of the French capital. Johann Strauss arrived from Vienna to present his newest waltz *On the Beautiful Blue Danube* to thrilled audiences. The most important opera nights were no doubt both spring premieres: On 11 March the Opéra premiered Verdi's newest work, *Don Carlos*, in French, based on Schiller's play of the same name. Méry had died before finishing the libretto and Camille du Locle, a clerk at the Opéra and the son-in-law of its director Émile Perrin, had completed it. In *Don Carlos* Verdi tried to fulfill the demands of the five-act grand opera and its obligatory ballet segment. Internationally (and subsequently also in France), Verdi's authorized Italian version—without the ballet—was more successful. Bizet's judgment was harsh: "I adore *La traviata* and *Rigoletto*, but *Don Carlos* is a trade-off. No melody, no expression; it strives for style, but only strives. It made a disastrous impression. It is an utter failure. For the sake of the World Fair it might be claimed half-successful, but nonetheless, for Verdi it's a disaster."[12]

The other premiere that spring was a stunning success: Gounod's opera *Roméo et Juliette* was premiered on 27 April 1867 at the Théâtre Lyrique and has since then remained a lasting element in the repertoires of French opera houses, although in contrast to *Faust* (called *Margarethe* in Germany), it is rarely staged abroad. Bizet was directly involved in this success for his fatherly friend, whom he considered "the most perfect French composer";[13] he had written the piano score for Éditions Choudens.

For a different reason, however, he had less cause to rejoice over Gounod's success because it postponed the subsequent premiere at the Théâtre Lyrique, *La Jolie fille de Perth*. But Bizet's opera had to be postponed again anyway, because not only Nilsson, but the tenor, too, was no longer available. Bizet himself went to Bordeaux to see whether singer Massy was up to the part of Henry Smith. It was the second time since his return from Rome that he left Paris. Since his short visit to Baden-Baden five years previously he had never again been outside his hometown.

The World Fair presented an occasion for several contests. The prize money enticed Bizet to participate (although he was skeptical enough to use a pseudonym) in two competitions, entering a hymn for one and a cantata for the other. Neither piece gained any recognition; both have been lost. The circumstances surrounding these contests were vague to say the least. Composers from the most diverse of genres participated. One of the few serious pieces (and that still exists) was Camille Saint-Saëns's cantata *Les Noces de Prométhée* (Prometheus's Wedding).

Bizet continued to give lessons (among others, to Paul Lacombe from Carcassonne, an almost-same-age son of a factory owner) and also wrote a piano arrangement for Thomas's *Mignon*. He helped Saint-Saëns (who was three years his senior) write a piano score for the opera *Le Timbre d'Argent* (The Silver Bell) that was already finished for a libretto by Barbier and Carré, but that for the time being had no chance of being premiered. *Samson and Delilah*, Saint-Saëns's only other opera that is still well known today, was already finished but had not yet been performed. Finally, in the summer of 1867 rehearsals began for *Jolie fille*. About that time, Bizet met Henri Regnault, a young painter who had returned to Paris for a while after having also stayed, as a winner of the Prix de Rome, at the Villa Medici. Regnault's pictures reflected his impressions from the Near and Far East, and for the coming year he had planned a trip to Spain with his colleague Georges Clairin.

Unlike other Parisian composers, Bizet had not yet acted as a music critic or journalist when an editor invited him to write an article for the *Revue Nationale et Étrangère*. Using the anagrammatic pseudonym Gaston de Betzi, Bizet wrote one single article. He retracted a second article because he was

Poster by Éditions Choudens. *Bibliothèque Nationale, Paris*

unhappy with the editor's changes. He had never intended to be a man of letters anyway.

"A timid and blushing schoolgirl in her white ballroom dress is less ner-vous at her first waltz than I am at the prospect of seeing myself in print" was Bizet's apology to the reader in his first awkward attempt at journalism. And yet *Causerie musicale* ("musical chat," the title of his article published on 3 August 1867) is the passionate comment of a musician wanting to save music from being talked to death:

> We have French music, German music, Italian music . . . Russian music, Hungarian music, Polish music . . . Arab music, Japanese music, and Tunisian music . . . music of the future, music of the present and music of the past; . . . philosophical and ideological music . . . tomorrow we shall have needle music and screw music, force-pump music and double force-pump music. . . . For me there are only two kinds of music: good and bad. . . . A poet, painter, or musician . . . thinks, doubts, grows enthusiastic, despairs, rejoices and suffers in turn . . . he comes to us and says "Look and judge!" [but] instead of letting ourselves be moved, we ask him for his passport.[14]

That autumn Bizet wrote to Edmond Galabert: "I've met a wonderful girl. In two years she shall be my wife."[15] Bizet's wording is confusing; he was writing about Geneviève Halévy, who meanwhile had turned nineteen. Naturally he would have already known his teacher's daughter for a long

Geneviève Halévy. *Bibliothèque Nationale, Paris*

time. But now he was asking for her hand. Her mother was unhappy about it and opposed their engagement.

Much has been said about the widow's dismissive position. She can't have had reservations about her daughter marrying a musician and man of the theater, because Jacques Fromental himself, and his brother Léon, and his son Ludovic were all artists. Neither was Georges Bizet poor: not many could afford a home in the city and property just outside of town with two, albeit modest, houses on it. The social differences were thus not insurmountable. Bizet was considered a promising talent and was promoted by respected colleagues. His reputation was at the most a bit tainted by the existence of little Jean Reiter, assuming that anyone knew of the boy's true parentage. While Georges Bizet was a nonreligious humanist, that cannot have bothered the Halévys; they were liberal Frenchmen of Jewish origin. And in the country that invented civil marriage, unlike faiths cannot have posed a problem. Ever since her husband's and her daughter Esther's deaths, Hannah Léonie Halévy's relationship to her daughter Geneviève was strained. Hannah had become increasingly religious and suffered from mental disorders, and now her daughter Geneviève had begun exhibiting signs of the same. Madame Halévy also pedantically kept books on the royalties from her deceased husband's works and was perhaps very upset that Bizet had still not completed Halévy's opera Noé.

Finally Jolie fille was scheduled to show for the first time on 26 December 1867. But two weeks sooner the Théâtre Lyrique was to have another first showing, namely, Cardillac by August-Lucien Dautresme, based on material by E. T. A. Hoffmann. Forty-year-old Dautresme was another of the wealthy "semiprofessional" composers that competed with Bizet and his serious Parisian colleagues. Dautresme had been a marine engineer. He then devoted several years to music alone, and finally entered politics, becoming a left-party representative in the National Assembly, and eventually even the secretary of trade. Bizet spent the time until the premiere working on an odd-job composition. He, Léo Delibes, and two other composers each wrote one act for the operetta Marlborough s'en va-t-en guerre (Marlborough Has Left for the War). The humorous material dealt with the same milieu as Scribe's Le Verre d'eau (The Glass of Water): the English court of the early eighteenth century. In this historical persiflage à la Offenbach, Marlborough stays home from war to guard his wife's fidelity. The title was taken from the first line of a popular and much-cited ballad about the English general who fought Louis XIV.

Delibes, who was two years Bizet's senior, had been accepted at the Conservatoire the same year as Bizet and had also been a pupil under Adolphe Adam. As of 1865 he was the second choir director at the Paris Opéra, but he was unknown as a composer. The operetta composed by the four musicians was shown on 13 December 1867 at the Théâtre de l'Athénée, which had recently been bought by William Busnach, Madame Halévy's nephew. The Théâtre de l'Athénée had been built three years previously near the construction site of the new Opéra by Jewish patron Raphael Bischoffsheim, who used it mainly for concerts. It was on a street named after Eugène Scribe, who had died in 1861. Two of the other composers involved in writing the operetta for the Athénée were of Jewish descent: Émile Jonas and Isidore-Édouard Legouix. These circumstances may have convinced Bizet to collaborate on this "interim" project in order to placate his future mother-in-law. Unfortunately the entire production material for *Marlborough* has been lost.

The public and the press found the opening night of *Jolie fille* a respectable success. But the piece was performed less than twenty times and once again Carvalho had to save his house from bankruptcy by changing the program to increase proceeds. He tried it with Clapisson's *La Fanchonette*. But nothing helped; by May 1868 the Théâtre Lyrique was out of business. Léon Halévy is said to have offered Bizet a new libretto, *Le Templier*, based on Walter Scott's *Ivanhoe*. But in light of his recent experience with Scott motifs, and irrespective of the opinion of his future in-laws, Bizet turned the offer down.

Notes

1. *Le Château de Kenilworth ou le comte de Leicester* by Auber (1823), Donizetti's *Elisabetta al castello di Kenilworth* (1829), and *La Donna dellago* by Rossini (1819).

2. Jérôme von Gebsattel, *Kindlers Literatur Lexikon* (Munich, 1986), 9067.

3. Conducted by Georges Prêtre for Parthé Marconi/EMI.

4. Max Kalbeck, *Wiener Opernabende* (Berlin, n. d. [1885]), 190f.

5. Georges Bizet, *Lettres (1850–1875): Choisies et présentées par Claude Glayman* (Paris, 1989), 146.

6. A voice in a particularly high range named after French baritone Jean-Blaze Martin (1768–1837).

7. She had been triumphant in *La traviata* at the Théâtre Lyrique in 1864 and played later at the Opéra where she was the first Marguerite in Gounod's full musical version of *Faust*.

8. From a letter dated February 1894. Taken from *Hugo Wolfs Briefe an Melanie Köchert* (Tutzing, 1964).

9. Eduard Hanslick, "Aus meinem Leben," in Eduard Hanslick, *Vom Musikalisch-Schönen: Aufsätze und Musikkritiken*, ed. Klaus Mehner (Leipzig, 1982), 235.

10. Siegfried Kracauer, *Jacques Offenbach und das Paris seiner Zeit* (Frankfurt am Main, 1976), 159.

11. Kracauer, *Jacques Offenbach*, 159.

12. Bizet, *Lettres*, 158.

13. Bizet, *Lettres*, 119.

14. Dean, *Bizet* (London, 1975), 285.

15. Bizet, *Lettres*, 160.

CHAPTER ELEVEN

No New Opera, but Marriage and War, 1868–1871

In March 1868, the Paris Opéra staged *Hamlet* by Ambroise Thomas. Its sensational success was due especially to twenty-four-year-old Christine Nilsson singing the role of Ophelia. *Hamlet* remained on the program for decades and by the turn of the century had been shown more than three hundred times. Thomas made money off it and Bizet—who had otherwise not been particularly crowned by financial success—shared in the profits by writing piano scores: Heugel paid him nine hundred francs to write arrangements for four hands for three arias from *Hamlet*. Some consolation was to be had from the fact that in Brussels one of Europe's most modern and splendid opera houses, the Théatre de la Monnaie, reproduced *La Jolie fille de Perth*. Bizet went there for opening night in April, but was deeply disappointed with the performance. For a bit of distraction he visited Antwerp, did some sightseeing, and went to Brussels' museums. Never again during his lifetime were any of his works staged outside of Paris.

At that time, Bizet's health and mood were not the best. He was tempted to disavow independence and take on any available office, particularly because he wanted to marry. Colds and sore throats beset him time and again. He mentions symptoms in his correspondence, but never speaks of medical consultation or treatment. Claude Glayman believes that having not cured the illness, Bizet suffered from "maladie dite de Bouillaud," a kind of joint rheumatism with serious complications.[1] Bizet ignored his discomfort, the more so as it did not really impede his work. He pulled out the score for his *Roma* symphony again and completed what he had begun in Italy ten years earlier. During the summer at Le Vésinet he also wrote two new pieces for the piano.

After first composing a little *Nocturne*, in July 1868 he then began writing his longest, and at the same time, his last solo music for the instrument on which he had started, the piano. He dedicated these *Variations chromatiques* to Stephen Heller, the famous Hungarian pianist and friend of Chopin who at the time was teaching in Paris. The theme and most of the fourteen variations, half of them in C major and the other half in C minor, are peculiarly inconsistent.

On the one hand, here the composer appears to explore new territory in melody and harmony, but on the other hand the work includes traits typical of virtuoso salon music. The theme sounds like a funeral march, and the chromatics is repeated by a lament bass figure, as was common for Baroque music. The polonaise variation and one passage with opera-like tremolos both seem to be foreign matter in this overall enigmatic piece, whose occasionally aggressive expression seems directed inward. The work does not seem particularly eclectic. We do not know whether Heller ever performed Bizet's *Variations chromatiques*. Bizet himself did not play them until 1871 at one of his ever less frequent piano performances.

These *Variations*, which were not only unusual for Bizet, but for the entire repertoire of piano music at all, have often aroused the interest of unusual pianists. Glenn Gould made a recording of them. Felix von Weingartner, the first conductor to perform Bizet's symphony, published a new edition of the *Variations* in 1933 and also wrote the score for an orchestra version of them.

In the summer of 1867 all three opera theaters in Paris advertised their competitions in preparation for the World Fair. The Opéra was particularly thorough by starting with a call for librettos. It was not until April 1868 that they then made the call for composers to put music to the libretto they had chosen. At first Bizet encouraged his two correspondence pupils Galabert and Lacombe, who occasionally came to Paris, to try their luck. The libretto that won was *La Coupe du roi de Thulé* (The King of Thule's Goblet) by Louis Gallet and Édouard Blau. At the time, one of the most widely admired melodies from any opera was Gounod's aria "Il était un roi de Thulé" written for Marguerite in *Damnation of Faust*. Its popularity surely influenced the jury's decision in favor of this material and title.

The opera is about a descendant of the king of Thule, a legendary figure from a northern island that Goethe had made popular by a poem. The man dies out of love for a woman named Myrrha, and having no children, he has the goblet that guarantees power thrown into the sea. Yorick, who is also in love with Myrrha, retrieves the goblet, but gets neither Myrrha's hand nor the crown. The siren Claribel, who for her part is in love with Yorick, lets the entire royal court, Myrrha, and her lover Angus, perish by deluge.

Although reluctant after his experience with the contest a year before, Opéra director Perrin persuaded Bizet to compete for the prize. "If I enter the Opéra's contest and don't win, it might change my currently good situation for the worse. But if I won the prize, it might relieve me of pressing worries for two years. If I neither enter the contest nor master my big project, I'll be caught between the stools."[2] The "big project" was a new opera that he wanted Perrin to stage.

Eugenio Díaz de la Peña, an outsider and the son of a well-known painter, was obviously promoted and won the competition. The jury dismissed not only Bizet's score, but music by his friend Guiraud and a score by Jules Massenet as well. Massenet, who was four years younger than Bizet, had won the Prix de Rome in 1863 and had seen his own one-act piece *La Grand'tante* premiered at the Opéra Comique in April 1867. Within the context of the *Coupe* contest, Bizet wrote disparagingly to the wife of physician Ulysse Trélat: "This Massenet is terribly conniving, and I'm afraid of his many lies."[3] Bizet was at least spared seeing his late-bloomer colleague Massenet become hugely successful at the opera. Both had been guests at the home of Marie Trélat, an esteemed singer to whom both Bizet and Massenet dedicated songs.

Bizet's work on *La Coupe* had been in vain, then, because it was impossible to have his version performed anywhere else. He worked parts from his score into other works of his own. After Bizet's death, Choudens printed Bizet's *La Coupe* overture as a funeral march. Other individual songs from sections of the score that Bizet did not reuse were posthumously given new texts and published as *mélodies*. Eighty-six (for the most part loose) pages from the original score are archived at the National Library. Winton Dean tried to make performable music out of these approximately four hundred measures of notes by Bizet. In 1995 it was recorded and broadcasted by BBC London.

In late February 1869, Jules Étienne Pasdeloup performed *Roma* under the title "Fantaisie symphonique—Souvenirs de Rome," omitting the scherzo and playing only the three movements that had not yet been heard. The three movements had been given subtitles not authorized by Bizet. Pasdeloup took over directing the Théâtre Lyrique and staged Wagner's *Rienzi* there for the first time in Paris. Bizet witnessed one of the six-hour-long performances. It was an attempt by Pasdeloup to enhance the Théâtre Lyrique's profile by showing German grand opera. In contrast, the Paris Opéra was in the process of doing the opposite and was extremely successful at taking a piece shown in "comique" format at the Théâtre Lyrique and letting composers make grand opera out of it. They did this, for example, for Gounod's *Faust* by adding a ballet segment and several songs that soon became very popular. It became the version of *Faust* that is today played internationally. Recitatives replaced the spoken dialogues typical of an opera comique; that was a *conditio sine qua non* at the house on rue Lepeletier. Even in 1842 Weber's Freischütz had not been performed in its original form: Hector Berlioz had to compose recitatives for it.

On 8 March, Hector Berlioz died at the age of sixty-five after a severe illness. He was ceremoniously brought to his grave at Montmartre. The city's important musicians attended, and Bizet was among them.

On 14 May 1869 Bizet mentioned in a letter to Galabert that he would now actually marry Geneviève Halévy. Meanwhile the little daughter of his teacher for composition had become a pretty young lady. She had long brown hair, large dark eyes, and voluptuous lips. (No prenuptial pictures exist, but later portraits confirm this description by her peers.) Geneviève expected a sense of security and balance from her marriage to the serious young composer, but also liberation from her mother Hannah Léonie. For years she had not lived with her mother, but with relatives instead.

To the satisfaction of his future mother-in-law, Bizet now finally began completing Halévy's opera *Noé*. He used notes from *Vasco da Gama* and *Ivan IV* to do so. Neither he nor his mother-in-law lived to see *Noé*'s premiere in Karlsruhe in 1886. In France, Halévy's posthumous work with

Cover page of the piano score for Halévy's opera *Noé* that Bizet completed

Bizet's additions was not shown until 2004, when it was staged by the Théâtre Imperial in Compiègne.

Hannah Léonie Halévy could not attend the couple's civil marriage ceremony because she was curing a nervous disorder at a sanatorium in Ivry-sur-Seine. They had no church ceremony. Georges and Geneviève Bizet spent their honeymoon at the country home of her uncle Hippolyte Rodrigues in Saint-Gratien in the valley of Oise north of Paris. He was the only one from the Rodrigues family that from the start approved of their union. Hippolyte Rodrigues (1812–1898) had been a successful exchange broker who after retirement pursued literary and musical interests. He published a collection of Jewish songs (*Apologues de Talmud*) and had already written music for an opera (*David Rizzio*, based on the life of that musician, a favorite of Maria Stuart).

At summer's end Georges and Geneviève Bizet moved into their city dwelling at rue de Douai no. 22, where Ludovic Halévy also lived. It was just a few steps from Bizet's father's home on rue Fontaine, and just a few streets from the house Georges was born in on rue de la Tour d'Auvergne. Bizet spent almost his entire life in the same neighborhood near Place Pigalle.

On 17 November 1869 a French ship with Empress Eugénie on board was the first to pass through the Suez Canal, built by the Frenchman Ferdinand de Lesseps. Once more, Napoleon III presented himself and his country to the world as an engine for civilization and progress. The likewise newly established opera house in Cairo had just opened with Giuseppe Verdi's *Rigoletto*. Through Camille du Locle, who had meanwhile become the director of the Opéra Comique, Verdi landed a commission from the opera-loving Egyptian viceroy to write an opera based on an Egyptian topic. But the political confrontation between France and Germany postponed premiering *Aida* until Christmas 1871.

In early 1870 Bizet had new opera plans. His remaining papers include sketches for *Grisélidis* and a Boccaccio adaptation by Victorien Sardou. The latter was a successful theater writer at the time; his drama *La Tosca* is still familiar today through Puccini's opera. Bizet also considered writing music for Samuel Richardson's *Clarissa Harlowe*, no doubt colorful material for an opera. He also thought of doing a Gallic *Vercingétorix*, and *Rama*, an old story from India, and finally, prompted by Gounod's Mireille, perhaps also considered the Provençal epic of *Calendau* by Frédéric Mistral. But none of these stories fascinated him enough to make him willing to do serious work without a contract. And everyday life was becoming increasingly threatened by politics: tension had mounted between France and Prussia. Bizet was a realistic person and cognizant of current events. Originally he had planned to spend the summer in the country with Geneviève, working in peace. But news of the outbreak of war let the couple return to town immediately. Prosper Mérimée, who over the years had become a confidant and literary advisor for the French empress, described the mood of summer 1870: "Everyone is frightened, without quite knowing why. Overall everyone is anxious and nervous. It feels like the last act from Mozart's *Don Juan*, before the commander appears. . . ."[4]

France's inglorious involvement in Mexico and the consequences of the war between Austria and Prussia had considerably damaged Napoleon III's standing. The emperor tried to stabilize things at home by allowing people to move more freely and by introducing a constitutional monarchy as it were. After allowing his subjects to vote on the constitution, he considered his position secure. But at court a circle of corrupt speculators had grown that estranged the government from the people. They ordered the production of the first machine guns, so-called *mitrailleuses*, and expanded the railway to the north. The Prussians had already strategically laid rails in France's direction. The French emperor hoped for solidarity from Austria (though weakened after the defeat at Sadowa) and from Italy (whose king he had helped claim the throne but then had left dangling by also supporting the pope). Napoleon III played up the question of Prussia's influence ending at the Main River and on 19 July 1870 declared war on Prussia. The welcome pretense for doing so were rumors that Prussian prince Leopold from the House of Hohenzollern-Sigmaringen would be heir to the throne in Spain.

In Bad Ems on the river Lahn, where Wilhelm I had just attended a performance of *La Chanson de Fortunio* directed in French by Jacques Offenbach himself, the French ambassador demanded from the Prussian king that Prince Leopold renounce any claim to the throne in Spain, a matter that had actually already been settled anyway. Wilhelm I initially refused, and by making it public through the Ems Dispatch, Bismarck accelerated the war.

After returning to the city, Georges Bizet joined the militia, the Garde Nationale. As a winner of the Prix de Rome he was exempt of any military duty. "Today we must rescue the country! But then what? What about our poor philosophy and our dream of universal peace, what about cosmopolitan brotherhood and human communion? . . . Instead: tears, blood, and shredded flesh, crimes without end! Dear friend, I cannot say how all of this saddens me. I'm a Frenchman, I know, but can I forget that I'm human?"[5]

On 1 September Napoleon III capitulated after the battle at Sedan. The emperor was taken prisoner by the Prussians, and in Paris the nation was proclaimed a republic. The new government continued the war. On 19 September Paris was surrounded by Prussian troops. Because of the war, Prosper Mérimée, who besides his friendship with the court had also for many years been the inspector of historical monuments, retreated to Cannes. He died

Bizet as National Guardsman

there on 23 September, shortly before his sixty-seventh birthday; the news of the emperor's defeat and the occupation of Paris were too much for the author already marked by illness.

Like Bizet, a young writer from Nîmes had also served in the National Guard and had collected and written down his impressions of the capital under siege: in a mixture of report and satire Alphonse Daudet recollects how "the inhabit-

ants of Paris will never again be able to see the inevitable tin can without thinking of their five-month-long blockade" . . . and how a senile colonel (whose
family, in an attempt to prevent him from having another stroke, pretends that
French troops are victoriously marching to Paris) tells his granddaughter about
Napoleon I's march to Moscow: "Imagine that! We ate horsemeat! Of course
she could imagine it, for two months there had been no other meat." Montmartre he described as "a big village, armed to the teeth, machine guns at the rim
of the watering place, the church grounds teeming with bayonets, a barricade in
front of the school . . . every house turned into a casern."[6] German soldiers stole
a pendulum clock in the suburb of Bougival and took it to Munich. In Daudet's
version of the story the clock ends up in the possession of Bavaria's King Ludwig
II, who then no longer has Wagner's *Meistersinger* score laying out on his piano,
but instead *Le Phoque à ventre blanc* (The White-Belly Seal), an operetta with
music by Georges Douay written for a text by William Busnach that had been
a huge success at the Alcazar in Paris in July 1871.

Bloody battles took innumerous lives until on 18 January 1871 in Versailles
the Prussian king Wilhelm I was proclaimed German kaiser. In Paris a revolutionary central committee grabbed the power after communists and socialists
had rebelled against the bourgeoisie, whom they held responsible for the defeat.
Painters Manet and Courbet and author Émile Zola professed to be leftist. From
the isle of Guernsey Victor Hugo had called to continue fighting the Germans;
meanwhile he was a member of the National Assembly that convened in Bordeaux. At one time Hugo had supported the kaiser's claim to the Rhine.

We have no indication that any of the renowned musicians of the time
raised their voices on political matters. In February the Bizets went to Bordeaux to visit Geneviève's mother who now lived there with Rodrigues. The
two women had not seen each other since the time of the wedding, when
Madame Hannah Léonie had been in safe custody in Ivry. Following their
encounter in February, Geneviève had a mental breakdown.

Notes

1. Claude Glayman's foreword in Georges Bizet, *Lettres (1850–1875): Choisies et
présentées par Claude Glayman* (Paris, 1989), 12.

2. Bizet, *Lettres*, 168.

3. Bizet, *Lettres*, 272.

4. Prosper Mérimée, *Lettres a M. Panizzi* (Paris, 1881). Taken from Otto Zierer,
Neue Weltgeschichte (Stuttgart, 1966), 3:260.

5. Bizet, *Lettres*, 187.

6. Alphonse Daudet, *Montagsgeschichten*, trans. into German by Liselotte Ronte
(Munich, 1981), 38f.

CHAPTER TWELVE

Masterpieces—*Jeux d'enfants* and *Djamileh*, 1871–1872

Georges Bizet escaped the dreadful situation in the city by staying in Le Vésinet and working there. Thousands died in the streets of Paris before General Patrice de Mac-Mahon (who had led the army to victory against Austria in Magenta in 1859 and who later became president) put an end to the days of the Paris Commune. Many of Bizet's letters from that period tell of shock, distress, and violence. But not once does Bizet comment on politics.

In early July he returned to Paris. Under some pressure from his mother-in-law, he considered applying for the position of *chef de chant* at the Opéra, but the many official demands of the job would have kept him from composing. Dean finds reason to believe that Bizet did work there as choir director unofficially.[1] Besides money coming in from his own works, Bizet earned what he needed for a living by writing arrangements and commissioned pieces at home, independent of cooperation with others.

At the age of almost sixty, Ambroise Thomas followed Auber as the director of the Conservatoire. Shortly before Auber died at the age of eighty-nine in May 1871, the Paris Commune had ousted him for a few days.

Because of the overall situation, the Opéra Comique could not see itself producing a new evening-long opera like Bizet's *Grisélidis*. In compensation, du Locle and his codirector Adolphe de Leuven suggested that the disappointed composer write a one-act piece based on *Namouna* by Alfred de Musset, one part of a trilogy of closet dramas called *Un Spectacle dans un fauteuil* (Armchair Plays) published in 1832. Under the title *Djamileh*, du Locle had originally intended this libretto by Louis Gallet for another composer who was late in delivering. The two directors were in a hurry; just a few months were left before rehearsals were to begin.

The same opera house was already preparing other material by Alfred de Musset. Musset's brother Paul had written a libretto for Offenbach for the musical comedy *Fantasio* that premiered on 18 January 1872. Offenbach dedicated the score to Eduard Hanslick, who had supported his success in Vienna.

But before he could begin writing new music for the stage, Bizet had to complete a piano duet ordered by publisher Durand. In early 1872 it appeared as *Jeux d'enfants* (Children's Games), inspired both programmatically and in style by Robert Schumann. In twelve miniatures of one to three minutes each, Bizet relates moments from childhood. Particularly *La Poupée* (The Doll) clearly reveals how the German model influenced the formation of Bizet's melody.

The dialogue-like structure of the theme from *Colin-maillard* (Blind Man's Bluff) is characteristic of Bizet's emulation of Schumann. Martin Cooper has suggested that Schumann observed children from an adult perspective, thereby adding musical significance to his *Scenes from Childhood*, but that Bizet, who by nature was less complex than Schumann, not only empathized with children but actually felt as a child would.[2] Not a single measure in Bizet's *Jeux d'enfants* shows epigonic eclecticism because Bizet's structural clarity and unbiased temperament transcend all reference to tradition. The sixth piece, *Trompette et tambour* (Trumpet and Drum) picks up the sound of the scene at the Kremlin Wall from *Ivan IV* that Bizet surely also devised at the piano. Originally it was to be titled *Tin Soldiers*. Shortly before publication, the title of another piece, *La Toupie d'Allemagne*, was changed into simply *La Toupie* (The [Spinning] Top).

Until then, the quality and significance of Bizet's works for the piano—perhaps with the exception of *Chromatic Variations*—had been marginal to both his own production and the usual repertoire for pianists; *Jeux d'enfants*, however, presents the epoch's most original new lighthearted work for four hands at the piano.

Bizet used five of the piece's movements to—perhaps simultaneously—create an orchestra version that was published as *Petite suite* and presented with utmost success to the public for the first time on 2 March 1873. Édouard Colonne conducted it on the first evening of a groundbreaking series of concerts at the Théâtre de l'Odéon that was to result in an important musical tradition for Paris. The closely interrelated parts of the program began with Mendelssohn's *Italian Symphony*; the evening ended with a suite movement by Ernest Guiraud. Bizet's *Petite suite* was the heart of the program, preceded by Schumann's *Dreaming* from *Scenes of Childhood*, and followed by Schubert's *Erlkönig* (Erlking), sung by Pauline Viardot.

Here we hear *Trumpet and Drum* again and see how the composer evermore carefully achieved the desired sound by molding the details of the vocal line and enhancing instrumental coloring. The score for *Petite suite* proves that in terms of instrumentation, Bizet can be seen as a legitimate successor of Berlioz and a forerunner of Maurice Ravel. In commenting on the history of how the work was received, Egon Voss said, "This little work that contains not one note too many (how often can anyone claim that?) is not taken quite seriously in Germany; it should be better known."[3] *Les Quatre coins* (Puss in the Corner), the sixth movement that Bizet instrumented, was not published together with the others and was probably played for the first time when Michel Plasson made a CD recording in Toulouse in 1992. Georges Bizet was probably not as pleased with the result of *Les Quatre coins* as he was with the other movements; it is very much made for the piano, and the orchestra version is considerably paler than the original.

Bizet's concise and transparent score for *Petite suite* put an end to widespread allegations that Bizet had become a Wagnerian. These grew from misunderstandings surrounding *Djamileh*, which was first shown on 22 May 1872.

During the war, Wagner, who in Paris had found appreciative colleagues, fanatic followers, and generous supporters, revealed a dark side of his personality through primitive and spiteful writing. It fed the dispute between Parisian Wagnerians and Wagner opponents even more. Not only did Wagner write a "libretto" in 1870 for an operetta titled *Capitulation*,[4] in which he derided the French musical scene; in January 1871 he also wrote *To the German Army Just outside Paris*: "The German watch now stands in France's conceited heart . . . with silent force / in pious chastity / fulfilling inconceivable deeds too great for you to ever understand. . . ."[5] Until then, Wagner had not had any substantial impact on French music. Massenet had not yet written his great works, and crucial French Wagner devotees like Albéric Magnard (1865–1914) had not yet emerged.

Ernest Reyer claimed that *Djamileh* sounded something like *Meistersinger*, which today we find difficult to understand. At the most he could have been alluding to one of the choir's fugato, but even in Wagner's opera itself that was only an imitated, not an original element of style. Bizet did possess the prelude from Wagner's score and had studied it. He certainly admired Wagner's artful employment of traditional forms and instrumentation; but he certainly did not intend to unravel form and traditional harmonic, as Wagner's *Tristan* had irritatingly done. The conspicuous chromatics of *Djamileh* is based on oriental melody. Hellmuth Christian Wolff, too, sees this one-act piece, "its chamber-musical and colorful instrumentation and songlike melody formation as a great contrast to Wagner."[6] In addition, the development of the tenor part in *Djamileh* strays from elegance and moves toward the more heroic type of voice used for Don José in *Carmen* and later found in the tenor roles of Italian verism; it is not a forerunner to the German heroic tenor.

Djamileh's stage atmosphere and tone reflect the mood one encountered those days in private salons and artistic circles of the French capital. Orientalism had increasingly become a form of escapism, a relief from the growing melancholy and decadent sentiment that flowed from the damage done to the Grande Nation's self-image.

The Sultan's Favorites, painting by Georges Clairin, 1875

Djamileh, whose original name in Spanish was "Namouna," is a slave and concubine of Haroun, an oriental playboy, who shuns commitment to any woman: "Je n'aime aucune femme au monde! J'aime l'amour!" After a while he gives each of his bed slaves a generous gift and replaces her with another. Djamileh, however, loves Haroun, and refuses to leave him. Veiled, she mingles among the women from whom he will make his next selection. When he realizes that he has chosen her a second time, Haroun finally begins to feel what Djamileh desires that he feel for her.

Here, again, Bizet makes no attempt to achieve any sense of authentic folklore. He creates a pan-oriental atmosphere not by way of illustration, but by an underlying melody in a tonal language appropriate for the text. According to scene directions, this one-act story takes place at a palace in Cairo, Egypt. But the only musical number from this opera to become fairly well known is an aria sung by the title heroine called *Ghazel*, which is a poetic form from Persian and Indian culture. In that aria Djamileh sings of legendary King Lahore, from an Indian saga. The monotone style of the *ghazel* is combined with a rhythm known from *hôtess arabe* (cf. music sample on page 74). The vocal part centers on an exotic melisma:

The introductory chorus by men on a ship that one would expect to be on the Nile is accompanied by a tambourine beating that same typical rhythm that in *Vasco da Gama* was supposed to be Portuguese and in *Ivan IV* was meant to be Bulgarian, although it actually somewhat resembles a mazurka. The typical feature of the song is that the timbre changes with the hues that Bizet achieves by adding a piano to the orchestra. Years later we find this again in Saint-Saëns's *Aquarium* from *Carnival of the Animals*. Outside Haroun's palace, palace master Splendiano presents a new group of female slaves. Here Bizet for the first time makes use of melodrama, taking musical ideas from his overture.

At the heart of the accusation of being Wagnerian was a phrase in Djamileh's complaint "Sans doute, l'heure est prochaine . . ." after she has promised Splendiano, who admires her, that she shall become his if her hope to be chosen again by Haroun should be disappointed.

But this seemingly *Tristan* chromatics is hardly more than a clever wink by the composer at the erotic constellation up on the stage. Within the wider context, it appears neither anticipated, nor does it have any consequences.

During Bizet's lifetime, *Djamileh* ran only eleven times at the Opéra Comique. It was shown together with Gounod's *Le Médecin malgré lui* (The Doctor in Spite of Himself) that was likewise incapable of filling an entire evening, but that Bizet very much appreciated. Gounod had remained in England, to where he had flown from the events of the war. It wasn't Bizet, but Bizet's mother-in-law that sent a copy of the *Djamileh* score to Gounod in London!

Not until the centenary of Bizet's birth did Paris rediscover *Djamileh*, which because of its congenial combination of conversation, atmosphere, and music only reveals its true charm to a French-speaking audience. And yet this one-act masterpiece had more success abroad, once Bizet had become famous for *Carmen*. As with Bizet's symphony *Roma*, it was Gustav Mahler who presented *Djamileh* to a wider public in Vienna in 1898. At that opportunity, Eduard Hanslick said that *Djamileh* possessed "a pleasant harmony and unity of style" and "even more delicate tonality, more distinguishing traits" than *Carmen*.[7]

Just three weeks after *Djamileh*, the next one-act piece based on a libretto by Louis Gallet was staged at the Opéra Comique: Camille Saint-Saëns's firstling *La Princesse jaune* (The Yellow Princess). And just a month before premiering *Djamileh*, Georges Bizet had seen singer Célestine Galli-Marié in the one-act piece *Le Passant* (The Passer-By) written by his fellow pupil from the conservatory and at the Villa Medici, Émile Paladilhe. A while earlier, she had sung the title role in Thomas's *Mignon*.

By year's end, thirty-year-old Massenet had his own first premiere at the same house; but like all other operas shown there that year, his *Don Cézar de Bazan*, too, was later forgotten. The only first staging from 1872 to have sustained success was Lecocq's *La Fille de Madame Angot* (The Daughter of Madame Angot) that found its way into the French repertoire for operetta by starting in Brussels. Meanwhile Bizet and Massenet were more relaxed in each other's company and even played four-handedly at Madame Trélat's salon; Bizet had come to respect the younger composer's work. One day Massenet sent Bizet a collection of six songs called *Poème du souvenir* to which Bizet replied that he found them exquisite, novel, and authentic and that he would say more, if the composer were "German, dead, or at least 90 years old and ill."[8]

Notes

1. *Groove's Dictionary of Music and Musicians* (London, 1980), 758.

2. Martin Cooper, *Georges Bizet* (London, 1938), 101.

3. *Der Konzertführer*, 446.

4. For *Capitulation* Wagner first used the pseudonym "Aristop. Hanes." Later (1873) it was included in volume 9 of his complete works, *Sämtliche Schriften und Dichtungen*, p. 3.

5. *An das deutsche Heer vor Paris:* "Die deutsche Wacht, da steht sie nun in Frankreichs eitlem Herzen . . . mit stiller Wucht / in frommer Zucht / vollbringt sie nie geahnte Thaten, zu groß für euch, nur ihren Sinn zu raten." Richard Wagner, *Gesammelte Schriften und Dichtungen* (Leipzig, 1907), 9:12.

6. H. Ch. Wolff, "Der Orient in der französischen Oper des 19. Jahrhunderts," in *Die couleur locale in der Oper des 19. Jahrhunderts*, ed. Heinz Becker (Regensburg, 1976), 380.

7. Eduard Hanslick, *Aus neuer und neuester Zeit* (Berlin, 1908), 119.

8. The date of the letter from Bizet to Jules Massenet is not precise, but from early 1870. Taken from Hervé Lacombe, *Georges Bizet: Naissance d'une identité créatrice* (Paris, 2000), 468.

CHAPTER THIRTEEN

Successful Music for a
Failed Play, 1872–1873

In the midsummer of 1872 Georges Bizet once more became a father. Geneviève, who had not only experienced and suffered under her mother's mental disposition, but apparently inherited the disorder as well, seems to have drawn strength from expecting her own child. Bizet's legitimate son Jacques was born on 10 July; his illegitimate son Jean continued to live with Marie Reiter at Adolphe Bizet's home.

Georges was busy with occasional compositions, giving lessons, and working on a new score for Carvalho. It was not an opera, but it was indeed entertaining music of a very special nature and he applied himself to the task. Clever at theater managing, Carvalho had regained a foothold and was now the director of the popular stage Théâtre du Vaudeville. The term "vaudeville" (from *voix de ville*) can perhaps best be translated as "popular song." Originally it designated a kind of song that later became the traditional closing song for comedy and opéra comique. In France "vaudeville" was also used pars pro toto for a certain kind of theater entertainment that included preludes, intermediate acts, choruses, and songs, but never individual solo roles.

Over the past years the Théâtre du Vaudeville (whose then fairly newly constructed building now houses the cinema Gaumont-Opéra on boulevard des Capucines) had produced several rather unsuccessful plays written by Alphonse Daudet, the meanwhile widely read author of *La Petite chose* and *Lettres de mon Moulin* (Letters from My Windmill), in collaboration with Ernest L'Épine, one of Bizet's acquaintances. Both served the patron Duke of Morny (1811–1865), to whom Daudet (at the recommendation of Empress

Eugénie, who enjoyed the young author's poetry) was appointed as a secretary. Ludovic Halévy, too, was promoted by this art-loving stepbrother of Napoleon III. But thirty-two-year-old Daudet had no luck as a dramatist; his strength lay in describing milieus and times, particularly using stories from his homeland in Provence. In 1872 he tried to finally achieve acclaim as an author for the stage by making a drama out of one especially well-received episode from his *Letters from My Windmill*. The short version of *L'Arlésienne* was not even five pages long. It is the story of a nameless city girl from Arles whom Jan, an attractive and spirited farm boy from the region of Camargue, loves and desires to marry. But his family has moral objections. It turns out that the girl from Arles already has a relationship with another man who insists on marrying her and plans to abduct her. Jan commits suicide.

Alphonse Daudet, photograph by Nadar

Carvalho liked the idea of using this well-tried narrative a second time. Ever since Gounod's *Mireille*, using Provence for a setting was sure to arouse an audience's curiosity. Elements of folklore, especially the farandole dance, were very popular and according to Winton Dean, for Parisians settings south of Arles were almost as foreign as Egypt and Spain.[1] Bizet had once told Carvalho of the impressions he had gotten of Provence on his way to Rome, and now the theater man contracted him to write stage music for *L'Arlésienne*.

Daudet furnished the story he had published three years before with a few new characters. He contrasted the mysterious girl from Arles—who never appears on stage—with Vivette, an obvious country girl who wants to marry Frédéri (the new name for Jan), who is hopelessly in love with the city girl. For the stage a mentally disabled younger brother, mentioned only in passing in the short story, becomes the psychologically key figure *L'Innocent*. Bizet wrote a prelude, entr'acte, and finale (each enhanced by a short choir movement) for each of the five scenes of Daudet's three-act piece. Only one single musical episode, a berceuse for the little Innocent, is actually motivated by the story line.

Finances permitted only twenty-six orchestra musicians. Bizet made that serve his own extraordinary sense of instrumentation. With the unusual combination of four first and three second violins, one viola, but five cellos and one contrabass, a piano and a harmonium plus kettledrums and a tambourine, he achieved an unmistakable tone coloring for *L'Arlésienne*, accenting it further not only by the usual winds, but by a saxophone as well. The instrument invented by the Belgian instrument maker Adolphe Sax, who had worked in Paris since 1842, was already widely in use for French military music, but despite Berlioz and Thomas, one rarely heard it at the concert hall or from the orchestra pit.

Carvalho was probably particularly pleased with the first two-part prelude because vaudeville audiences were not particularly interested in musical innovation; they wanted catchy tunes that they might even already know from other contexts. Bizet reworked *Marche des Rois*, a song for Epiphany, making it, as it were, a colorful variation on the original theme.

The tune that became known as *Marche de Turenne* is—like all other melodies borrowed from other sources for the work—said to have its origin in Provence. The rhythmically resolute and clearly structured introduction is followed by an elegiac passage where an alto saxophone presents a musical thought (originally intended for *Grisélidis*) that is typically woven into the string movement. Bizet then unfolds a broad attenuated tutti phrase that can be seen as a model for subsequent orchestra episodes of the verists Leoncavallo and Puccini. The prelude for the third scene of *L'Arlésienne* was likewise probably made out of material originally intended for an opera. The introductory measures in unison and songlike theme would suggest it. At some later time someone used this music for *Agnus Dei*, letting many a church musician believe that Bizet was the author of musical sacral kitsch, as they were used to *Largo* from Handel's lighthearted opera about Xerxes the king of Persia being inappropriately mistaken by many for church music. *L'Arlésienne* has about twelve melodramatic passages, but none of them compare to Bizet's first attempts at melodrama in *Djamileh* or the melodrama of *Carmen*.

L'Arlésienne's premiere on 1 October 1872 at the Théâtre du Vaudeville flopped; the farandole used for a smashing finale could not alter that. Below one can see the characteristic sound of the two traditional Provençal folk instruments, the tambourine and the *galoubet* (a simple flute), that were played by one person holding one instrument in each hand.

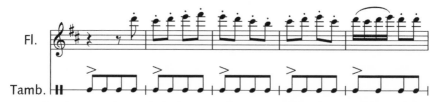

Until his death in 1897, Alphonse Daudet never again wrote anything for the stage. After *L'Arlésienne*'s failure, he even took a piece he had begun writing for the theater and changed it into a novel. Pasdeloup, however, was convinced that Bizet's preludes and entr'actes were of a superior quality and on 10 November he had them performed as a suite at the Cirque d'Hiver. An enthusiastic audience applauded Bizet. But that evening also marked the beginning of a series of misunderstandings. Pasdeloup's compilation, which quickly became popular as the First Arlésienne Suite, was played by a full symphony orchestra. But the distinctly delicate features of the original instrumentation are lost when, for example, the alto saxophone and five cellos are contrasted not by one single viola, but by a whole viola section. The misinterpretations continued when after Bizet's death Ernest Guiraud compiled a Second Arlésienne Suite that included music from *La Jolie fille de Perth*.

The music for *L'Arlésienne* was turned into a broad philharmonic sound using up to five times more musicians than originally intended. English conductor John Eliot Gardiner[2] wrote that Bizet felt inspired, not restricted by the small number of musicians at his disposal. Gardiner always sensed that something was wrong about the two Arlésienne suites: even when performed by the world's best orchestras, there is something peculiar about them; they are not the authentic handwriting of the composer that wrote *Carmen*. In the 1980s Gardiner and his colleague Michel Plasson were the first to perform the music from *L'Arlésienne* as originally intended for twenty-six musicians.

Bizet's popular melodies promoted Daudet's play and one occasionally finds it performed in France. In 1995 Swiss French radio produced a complete recording of *L'Arlésienne* taken from a stage performance in Mézières near Lausanne. It appeared under the Swiss label GALLO, whose CD edition of Bizet's music presents it in a dramaturgically authentic context with the original instrumentation. Three years later Germany's Westdeutscher Rundfunk produced a version of it in German but used narratives in place of scenes that are without music.[3]

The music to the failed play became an extraordinary success for its composer. During Bizet's lifetime, Pasdeloup conducted the suite from *L'Arlésienne* four more times at his Concerts Populaires, various pianists performed a piano arrangement, and between November 1873 and 1875 even Édouard Colonne had them on his program six times. A month before Bizet's death Édouard Deldevez conducted the suite twice within a series of concerts at the Société des Concerts du Conservatoire, where he sat on the board.[4] *Tout Paris* took note of it, even the directors of the Opéra Comique: De Leuven and du Locle ordered a new piece from Bizet. In one of his last letters to Galabert, who was still a full-time wine dealer in Montauban (southwest France), Bizet wrote on 17 July 1872 of a libretto by Ludovic Halévy and Henri Meilhac. Meilhac and Halévy had not only written libretti for Offenbach, they had also written humorous pieces like *Le Réveillon*, which was soon used as a model for Johann Strauss's *Fledermaus*. The great days of comic opera à la Offenbach were over; the empire no longer existed as a target for clever innuendos with musical esprit.

We do not know whose idea it was to use Mérimée's novella *Carmen* as material for a new opera; perhaps it was one of the directors', perhaps one of the librettists', perhaps Bizet's own idea. Surely they all knew the story of soldier Don José's tragic love for the tobacco factory worker Carmen, which

Henri Meilhac. *Bibliothèque Nationale, Paris*

Ludovic Halévy. *Bibliothèque Nationale, Paris*

since its first publication in 1845 had been one of the most popular French novels.

Bizet was quite confident: here was a fascinating story with interesting characters, charming settings, and finally two highly competent text writers, whose instinct for the theater, style, and cooperation he could trust. This time he had no reason to fear the discrepancies of cliché orientalism and true expression, vitality on the stage and dialogue needs, the meaning of the story and whether it could be sung—all the things that until then had hindered him in fully developing his composer imagination and his musical skill at opera.

He worked on *Carmen* much longer than he had on any other opera. In part that was because he also had other orders to fulfill, which he could not turn down. In the fall of 1872 Charles Gounod, who remained in London although the war was long over (and the French emperor himself lived in English exile), asked Bizet to supervise rehearsals for *Romeo et Juliette*. The work was scheduled for the Opéra Comique's program for January of the next year. On 9 January 1873, not far from Britain's capital, Napoleon III died.

Singer Jean-Baptiste Faure came to Bizet in the summer of 1873 to suggest (not entirely unselfishly) music for a new opera that he wanted to see performed at the Opéra. The suggestion was indeed promising because Faure was very influential. He was the leading baritone at the Opéra, and having had training in conducting, he knew the métier well. Faure had successfully sung Rossini's and Verdi's great parts for baritones, had shaped the title role in Thomas's *Hamlet*, and now wanted to be the center of attention in a new major role. But works with an attractive, central baritone role that might be appropriate for the Opéra and had not yet been staged there were difficult to find. Faure's idea was to seek out a composer and have him tailor a role to fit him.

Faure, however, had not yet negotiated with Olivier Halanzier-Dufresnoy, the director of the Opéra whose new building was not yet completed, that the work would actually be staged.

Faure wanted Louis Gallet and Édouard Blau to write the libretto; he was familiar with their work *La Coupe du Rois de Thulé*. Their first suggestion was to use Alfred de Musset's *Lorenzaccio*. Bizet would have liked to do it,

Jean-Baptiste Faure as Hamlet, 1868

but Faure found the character of Lorenzo di Medici cynical and unappealing. Bizet said of Faure's vanity: "Not only must he be great, handsome, generous and strong, but the other characters must be praising him when he's not on stage."[5]

Finally they agreed on a different historical figure from world literature that came closer to Faure's expectations: Don Rodrigo Díaz de Vivar, the Castilian grandee called El Cid, from the early eleventh century. The model for Blau and Gallet's libretto *Don Rodrigue* was not the familiar *Le Cid* drama by Corneille, but instead the play *The Deeds of Young Cid* by Guillén de Castro y Bellvís. Within a few weeks Bizet had outlined the singing parts for the entire work and presented some of it at home to a small circle of friends, improvising at the piano.

On 28 October 1873 the Opéra on rue Lepeletier burned to the ground. The new Palais Garnier was not scheduled to open until early the next year, so in the meantime performances were given provisionally at the Salle Ventadour. But despite Faure's intervention, Halanzier decided not to risk a premiere that might ignore petrified traditions at the Opéra. Bizet's opera on Spanish Don Rodrigo never got past the detailed outline, and he went back to work on *Carmen*.

Bizet was to work once more with Gallet. Inspired by Jules Massenet's success with the oratorio *Marie-Madeleine*, they had an idea for a dramatic legend called *Geneviève in Paris*, but never got around to writing the music for it. Blau and Gallet later returned to the *Don Rodrigue* libretto when working on their *Cid* opera for Massenet.

After having had great success with his opera comique *Madame Turlupin* at the Athénée in 1872, in May 1873 Ernest Guiraud saw the production of his one-act ballet *Gretna Green* at the Opéra. Immediately afterward, Pasdeloup commissioned Massenet, Guiraud, and Bizet to each write an *ouverture de concert* for his concert series.

These late-nineteenth-century concert overtures with their programmatic titles stood alone, without belonging to any comprehensive work. In other words, they were actually symphonic poems. Of the three final products, eventually only Guiraud's bore the expressed title of "ouverture de concert," and did so only provisionally, because he later renamed it after a Flemish folk hero, *Overture d'Arteveld*. Massenet wrote a *Phaedra* overture, probably referring to Racine; Bizet called his score *"Patrie!..."* The title is puzzling. Contemporaries may have seen some connection with Victorien Sardou's stage play of the same name about a sixteenth-century peasant uprising in the Netherlands. In fact, shortly after the war Bizet had spent some time with Sardou at his country home in Port Marly, working on the libretto for

Grisélidis, which they later discarded. *Patrie!...* may have been Bizet's way of underscoring their friendship.

Without authorization, and possibly inserted by Choudens for diplomatic business reasons, a subtitle appeared on the later published four-hand piano arrangement for *Patrie!...* that read: "Épisode de la guerre de Pologne (Bataille de Racławice gagnée sur les russes, par Kosciusko, 1792)." Bizet's first biographer picked up the reference without mentioning that it matched neither the manuscript, nor the first printing of the score.[6] (To boot, the Battle of Racławice did not seal the division of Poland until 1794.)

But the display of a patriotic attitude might also have simply been a clever tribute to the sentiments of postwar French audiences. The calculation, if indeed it was such, worked. The premiere of Bizet's *Patrie!...* on 15 February

Rue de Douai 22, Bizet's home in Paris.
Courtesy of C. Schwandt

1874 got thick applause. That is understandable because if performed brilliantly, it is an effective symphonic showpiece. But the musical substance is thin. It was an odd job done for the money; Bizet needed money because *Don Rodrigue* brought no income. *Patrie!...* is a conventional potpourri overture that contains thematic material from the opera Bizet had just outlined, including ideas worthy of further development that given better circumstances, Bizet surely would have reworked for better results.

The temperamental beginning of *Patrie!...* (tellingly dedicated to Massenet) reminds us of the "Racoczy March" in Berlioz's *Damnation of Faust*; the ending, full of pathos, is marked by superficial monumentality that seems foreign to Bizet's nature. Mina Curtiss diagnosed this last work that Bizet published before *Carmen* as revealing the weak side of Bizet's eclecticism,[7] and Dean writes it off as simply Bizet's "feeblest" work.[8]

Notes

1. Dean, *Bizet* (London, 1975), 202n1.
2. Text for the record cover ECD 75385.
3. It appeared as a CD under the label CAPRICCIO.
4. According to a list in Hervé Lacombe, *Georges Bizet: Naissance d'une identité créatrice* (Paris, 2000), 807f.
5. Dean, *Bizet* (London, 1975), 106.
6. Charles Pigot, *Georges Bizet et son œuvre* (Paris, 1886), 190.
7. Mina Curtiss, *Bizet and His World* (New York, 1958), 355.
8. Dean, *Bizet* (1975, p. 108), 143.

CHAPTER FOURTEEN

Carmen, an Opéra Comique

In 1845 the French monthly literary and cultural magazine *Revue des deux mondes* published Prosper Mérimée's serialized novella *Carmen*. The story was about Don José Lizarrabengoa's disastrous love for a gypsy woman. While in prison in Córdoba awaiting his execution, José tells the story of his life:

He came from Basque landed gentry. Exiled from his homeland after a violent dispute, he enters military service in Seville and becomes a dragoon corporal. He gets orders to arrest a cigar factory worker, Carmen, for injuring another worker during a brawl. The shy soldier, who at first is not unduly interested in Carmen, gradually succumbs to her allure and neglects his duty: she escapes and he is demoted, even jailed for it. She has a rasp smuggled in to him, but he leaves it unused. After release he is ordered to guard a house while Carmen dances inside for his superior. Later the two meet secretly and make love. José is then involved in a duel over her and injured, but the other suitor, an officer, dies. Now there is no way back for José. Despite his insecurity he cannot leave Carmen, and together they join a group of smugglers. José then discovers that Carmen is already married to Garcia, the leader of the gang. Finally he finds Carmen in Gibraltar, where she has persuaded a new lover to do away with Garcia. José takes the elimination of Carmen's husband upon himself but insists on a duel instead of murder. He longs to begin a new life with Carmen in America, but she refuses. Meanwhile, she has fallen in love with bullfighter Lucas and follows him to a corrida in Córdoba. There José demands an explanation, wants proof of her love. But Carmen craves freedom and will not return to his arms, saying she would rather die. José kills Carmen, buries her in the woods, and turns himself in.

Du Locle's codirector de Leuven initially found this material too immoral. Opéra comiques did not have bloody endings. Auber's *Fra Diavolo* and Herold's *Zampa* were exceptions.

Working very closely with the composer, Meilhac and Halévy wrote a libretto nearly perfect in construction, and yet of poetic clarity and convincing dramatic stringency. The plot and the music went hand in hand to create suspense. "Hardly any other work from opera of that era," writes Walter Felsenstein, "has these careful harmonies and dynamic details created so exclusively for the story and expression on stage as Bizet's *Carmen*."[1] That is why *Carmen* is one of the few operas whose scenes have never been crudely overhauled.

Putting aside his Slavonic family name of Majak, Henri Meilhac (1831–1897) took on the name of a French town as his nom de plume. Of the two authors, Meilhac had the greater sense of humor and had worked previously as a humorous illustrator. His first experience with the musical theater was writing operetta texts for composer Louis Deffès in Bad Ems: in 1861 he wrote the text for *Le Café du Roi* and a year later the book for *Les Bourguignonnes*, shortly after his *L'Attaché d'ambassade* (later to become the model for Lehár's *Merry Widow*) had shown at the Théâtre du Vaudeville. Even after considerable success at his first cooperation with Halévy in 1864 writing *La belle Hélène* for Offenbach, Meilhac continued to work with other librettists like Cormon and Busnach.

After his patron Morny died, Ludovic Halévy (1833–1908) worked at the ministry of the interior and office for affairs with Algeria. But together with Meilhac he continued to write for the theater. Besides *Carmen*, they also jointly wrote one last text for Offenbach.[2]

While Mérimée's novella describes a disastrous relationship between a man and a woman and makes third parties marginal, the opera must bring those parties into focus to create greater contrast and give the protagonists more profile. Bizet, du Locle, and the librettists knew that *L'Arlésienne* had failed because it lacked the clarity engendered by using pairs of antagonistic figures.

The opera contrasts the Andalusian gypsy woman Carmen—with her dark hair and red skirt—with a naïve Basque peasant girl, Micaëla, with blond braids and a blue skirt. The opera drops José's rival from the novella, Carmen's husband. It would have been too confusing to have three men struggling for one woman's affection. Since the novella's bullfighter Lucas made a bolder figure for the stage, his traits and those of Carmen's husband Garcia were combined to create Escamillo, a torero. A lieutenant and a sergeant were added to evoke the milieu of the military. Carmen is given two young gypsy women, Frasquita and Mercédès, as companions, and surrounded by smugglers Dancaïre and Remendado, both clearly genre figures from opéra comique.

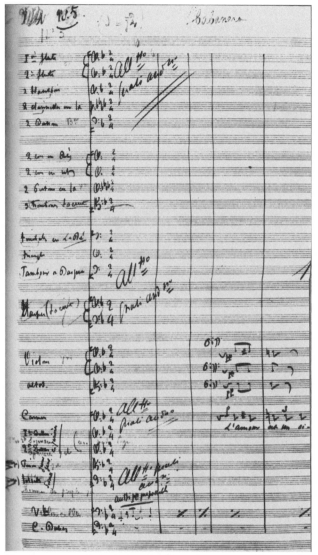

First measures of the habanera from the autograph score for *Carmen*

The libretto was finished by the summer of 1873. While writing the score, Bizet asked for changes to the text and made some alterations himself. Autograph documents show how carefully he balanced the lyrics with the music to achieve expression and proportion, particularly for Carmen's first song.

In September Marie Roze declined an offer to sing the title role. She hated the idea of the leading actress dying at the end of the story. She had not been the first choice anyway. Meanwhile, du Locle had become the sole manager of the Opéra Comique, once Adolphe de Leuven, the author of over 150 librettos and as old as the century itself, had retired. Du Locle initially wanted to engage Offenbach's buffa protagonist Zulma Bouffar for the role. But by the end of the year he had won Célestine Galli-Marié for the part. She was a great stage artist and a favorite with the Parisian audience, a fact that certainly motivated the composer and facilitated his surrender to the modifications she wished. Marie Célestine Galli-Marié must have had a relaxed, flexible mezzo soprano voice. She had sung the soubrette role of Serpina in Pergolesi's *La serva padrona* (The Servant

Célestine Galli-Marié, the first Carmen.

Turned Mistress) and is said to have asked du Locle to make her part in *Carmen* resemble Marguerite from Gounod's *Faust*. Carmen was thus written as a high mezzo soprano role for an experienced stage performer. (Deep alto and Wagner voices that later sang *Carmen* simply ignored the composer's original intention. Don José's part was similarly distorted by Italian and German heroic voices.)

During the summer of 1874 Bizet worked on a new score at Bougival, a suburb a few kilometers down the Seine near his father's summer cottage at Le Vésinet. This house lay idyllically surrounded by greenery with the river at the door. Today the town's main road goes right past it. The road has been named after Ivan Turgenev who at that time, like Madame Viardot and Ernest Guiraud, also lived in Bougival. That summer, publishers Michel Lévy Frères published the seventh edition of Mérimée's novella *Carmen*, which had sold well since it first appeared in 1846.

From time to time Geneviève Bizet lived separately from her husband, partly to allow him to concentrate on composing and partly due to her own health and that of her small son. The few extant letters suggest nothing of marital discord as so many have claimed. In terms of family background, life

The Seine near Bougival today; Bizet's house (the pointed roof in the center). *Courtesy of C. Schwandt*

experience, and habits, both Geneviève and Georges Bizet were very unconventional people. A lack of proof that their life as a couple did not match
the ideals of bourgeois mediocrity does not mean that their marriage was a
failure. And both living grandparents looked after their grandson Jacques;
at Adolph Bizet's home the youngest Bizet naturally played with his "half
uncle" Jean Reiter.

**Jacques Bizet and his grandmother Hannah Léonie Rodrigues-
Henriques, wife of Fromental Halévy and mother of Geneviève**

Despite the great effort put into it (and perhaps because Bizet no longer accepted urgent deadlines), the score that ultimately counted twelve hundred pages was not ready when rehearsals began on 1 May 1874. Bizet took recourse to sketches he had made for *Grisélidis*, for example, for shaping José's aria, which he had probably intended to do from the start, although he reworked the material so thoroughly that it probably saved him little time to use what he already had. Thinking that it was a folk song, Bizet borrowed the melody for Carmen's havanaise (habanera) from a song by Yradier (see page 72). He later explicitly corrected the error by adding an appropriate remark before the piano score was set for printing. The number actually fortifies the dramatic effect by letting the leading actress introduce herself with music immanent to the plot. Thus revised by Bizet, the song did eventually become very popular.

Rehearsals for *Carmen* did not begin until mid-November 1874. Bizet needed to revise once again, add here, delete there. The singers' requests were not the sole source of changes; unusual demands placed on the choir and orchestra were equally responsible.

Grand opening of the new opera house in Paris, Palais Garnier

The new Opéra was inaugurated on 5 January 1875, showing excerpts from various operas and ballets. The first entirely new opera to be produced at Palais Garnier was to be Reyer's *Érostrate*. This was a delicate matter because after scoring it the composer had dedicated the work to the queen of Prussia, who in turn decorated him with a medal, the Order of the Red Eagle. The Third Republic now treated itself to a representative monument planned by Napoleon III and Haussmann, the Palais Garnier, which in artistic terms was a relic of the past. But after the war, Paris was hardly republican; supported by monarchist forces, President Mac-Mahon bore the hope of restorative powers. France did not give itself a republican constitution until 1875.

On 15 January 1875, Antoine de Choudens made one of the most lucrative and prestigious deals in music publishing: he bought the score for *Carmen* from Bizet for twenty-five thousand francs. It was a respectable sum with a purchasing power comparable to more than sixty thousand euros today.

On 3 March the *Journal officiel* announced Bizet's decoration as chevalier of the Legion of Honor. That evening, *Carmen* was premiered. It has been said that du Locle made certain that the normal audience for premieres did not attend. He worried that the society that usually filled the seats on such special occasions would not appreciate the scandalous work. On premiere evenings, namely, the loges at the Opéra Comique were often the sites of matchmaking. An opera whose title heroine is a gypsy and factory worker, who persuades a soldier to desert and smuggle, who dances and sings in taverns, takes her fate into her own hands, and in the end is stabbed by her last lover on the open stage was the exact opposite of what people expected to see at the Opéra Comique. All figures in *Carmen* are ordinary people; there are no princesses, gods, spirits, or exotic Orientals. Don José personifies the collapse of bourgeois morals. An immature male protagonist, a village chap broken by the city's enticements, he was by no means a character one might identify with.

That evening at the Salle Favart, then, the majority of the audience was made up of friends of the author and the performers, many colleagues, and music experts. The show left them confused; their applause was reserved. Du Locle himself had undertaken the stage direction and Georges Clairin had designed the costumes. Clairin had traveled Spain with Henri Regnault and worked his impressions into the visual presentation of the story. Perhaps it would have been better for Bizet had his audience consisted of narrow-minded traditionalists booing in disgust. It might have sparked a more constructive debate on the innovative and provocative aspects of his work.

Some parts of the score, particularly the formal, conventional parts, did get considerable applause. Act 1 was a success. But in the end, the whole

Georges Bizet, about 1875

work was simply confusing. Bizet confronted old musical forms with new ones, and put dialogue and music in an unfamiliar relation to one another. He presented dissimilar ways of life, some tragic, others casual, within one and the same framework. But above all, it was novel to combine realistic elements with the overstylized stuffy manner of grand opéra.

More so than Verdi's operas that condense conflicts to their basic elements and force characters eventually to their limits, and more clearly than Wagner's musical drama that gives the plot momentum by an undertow of, for instance, the thought of redemption, *Carmen* shows man as always torn between two choices. Its whole music, its song and orchestra, do not merely express the feelings of the figures as they act and react, it also personifies the antagonistic outside forces working on the characters.

Carmen's instrumental opening is as stirring as it is brief: as in *Arlésienne*, it consists of a two-part prelude. In a somewhat potpourri style, Bizet frames the refrain for Escamillo's couplet with the spirited folk chorus music from the final scene. In dramatic tonal contrast (D minor follows A major like a movie scene cut), Bizet then introduces the opera's central musical idea, a short motif thoroughly shaped by a "touch of gypsy" contrasted with pizzicato syncopation, a stylistic device he had already tried for *The Pearl Fishers*. It grows ever more insistent over just twenty-eight measures and culminates in an abruptly diminished seventh chord. It is surely one of the most gripping and convincing beginnings of any opera.

Andante moderato

The curtain rises to reveal an everyday scene quite typical of opera comique: bored soldiers on guard watch passersby. Micaëla comes and asks about Don José before he has even entered the stage. Singing ragamuffins imitate the changing of the guard. José encounters Carmen as she sings her havanaise to admirers during her work break: "L'amour est un oiseau rebelle que nul ne peut apprivoiser. . . ." Micaëla returns with a letter from José's mother, imploring him to marry the village girl. Above all, it is the music that contrasts the two young women's expectations of life and love. Micaëla's entreating melody, reminiscent of sentiment from the *Pearl Fishers* duet, evokes in José a yearning for his mother and village back home.

A quarrel at the factory leads to violence, and José is ordered to arrest Carmen. With flirtatious warbling she first evades questioning by the lieutenant; then she beguiles José with a chanson, promising a rendezvous at a tavern. Here Bizet gives the music an original dramatic significance beyond what was common for serenades and otherwise purely entertaining songs at the opera. José lets Carmen escape. Bizet's music withdraws at exactly the right point in the drama and its indispensable dialogues. The later transformation of the work to a recitative edition destroyed precisely that clarity of dimension so important for act 1 of *Carmen*.

The music of the entr'acte reveals instrumental nuances of a fascinating simplicity that Bizet began to develop for *Ivan IV* and had fully mastered by the time he had completed the *Petite suite* and *L'Arlésienne*. The context surrounding the folk song–like melody is important for the drama. After spending time in jail, in act 2 Don José will once again enter the stage to precisely that melody. The quintet of three gypsy ladies and two smugglers, with its affective complexity and formal balance, is probably one of the most organic opera ensembles since Mozart.

Don José enters the tavern. There is something about him that Carmen likes (he's a "handsome guy") and she reconsiders going along with the smugglers. She sings and dances for him. The peak of tragic development in their relationship is expressed dialectically exclusively by the music when José must decide to either stay with Carmen or return to military duty. The trumpet calls, and he wants to return to the barracks. But then he argues with his superior, who also wants Carmen, and the course is set: José joins Carmen and the smugglers.

The atmosphere at the "wild, secluded cliff spot" in act 3 is a further development of the music for the Kremlin Wall scene in *Ivan IV*. Carmen scolds José: Go home to your mother! She reads her fortune from the cards. In an Offenbach-like trio, Carmen reads of her approaching death in a chant entirely different from the two other singing women, Frasquita and Mercédès, both of them swooning over prospects of husbands and riches. When they hear what Carmen has seen in the cards, they withdraw embarrassed, retreating in a manner from opera comique. Peter Brook and Marius Constant's version of *Carmen*[3] rightly synchronizes this gloomy cantilena with Micaëla's aria, which a few pages later in the score will express the village girl's fear of the strange woman that José desires.

Escamillo, who met Carmen in the tavern, now comes looking for her. Unaware that Don José is the other man in love with her, Escamillo tells Don José that he wants Carmen. Carmen prevents José from knifing Escamillo, and José returns to his mother together with Micaëla.

The entire opera takes place in Seville (the novella ends in Córdoba) and in act 4 at Seville's arena José and Carmen are finally alone. Meanwhile, her lover is Escamillo. A large scene shows the busy crowd before a bullfight.

Everyone has taken their place in the arena except Carmen and José outside the entrance. Inside the arena Escamillo kills a bull while outside the gate José kills Carmen after she throws down the ring he had given her. Bizet effectively plays out this dramatic synchrony in the score.

Some have said that after the performance Bizet withdrew to du Locle's office and then, as Halévy later reported, silently walked home with him and Meilhac; Pigot, on the other hand, writes that Guiraud said that they wandered the streets all night with the disappointed and angry composer. The reviews were anything but positive, and posterity has come to find them blindly reactionary and ridiculous. Even before its first showing, *Carmen* had polarized the cultural circles of Paris—or those who understood themselves as such—and afterward they poured out their resentment. But reviewers were not just music critics; many were highly partial and envious persons competing with the composer: for instance composer Ernest Reyer, and the publisher Léon Escudier, who aspired to directing a theater himself. Some exceptions were Victorin de Joncières, also a composer, and Théodore de Banville, an author uninvolved with Paris's musical theater scene. He found that Bizet, whom he considered a Wagnerian, had with the help of the orchestra put characters of real flesh and blood on the stage instead of the expected figures, the "decent bandits, crooning ladies, and rosewater-scented affairs." Bizet, du Locle, and the two librettists had "tossed all the old junk and ghosts of the Opéra Comique out the window."[4]

CARMEN

Opéra-Comique en quatre actes.

H. MEILHAC et L. HALÉVY.   MUSIQUE de GEORGES BIZET

The final scene of *Carmen* shown on the poster announcing the premiere, 1875. *Bibliothèque Nationale, Paris*

In April 1875 Vienna's office for court ceremonies named Franz von Jauner its new director for the Vienna Court Opera. Despite the cool reception in Paris, Jauner liked *Carmen* and wanted to show it in German in Vienna without fail. But he insisted that the score be cut and that a ballet be added to act 4. To make matters worse, the Vienna Court Opera accepted spoken dialogue only for *The Magic Flute*, *Fidelio*, and *The Marksman*; contemporary opera was supposed to be musical through and through. Although it depressed him, being the pragmatic realist that he was, Bizet agreed to revise *Carmen* and add recitatives. He signed the contract in early May.

But by the end of the month he was once again so ill with tonsillitis and rheumatism that he relocated his family to Bougival. As careless as he had been as a young man, he and the pianist Élie Miriam Delaborde went for a swim in the chilly Seine. The symptoms flared up again, this time with fever. At some time during the night before 1 June, Bizet collapsed. It was first interpreted as a heart attack, but in his last letters Bizet had complained of severe tinnitus, deafness in one ear, and loss of balance, symptoms that indicate neurological complications. Geneviève, Marie Reiter, both sons, and Geneviève's cousin, Ludovic Halévy, were all near. While talking with Marie, Bizet lost consciousness.

On his sixth wedding anniversary, 3 June 1875, Georges Bizet died at the age of thirty-six. That day, his opera was played for the thirty-third time at the Opéra Comique. Interest in *Carmen* grew. But many came simply to see something of a scandal at the theater. To improve the theater's finances, du Locle invited Verdi to alternately conduct seven performances of *Messa de Requiem* that a year before had made good money.

In October Vienna was sensationally successful with its premiere of *Carmen*. And within just a few years the work had become part of opera repertories in every language on all continents. But soon it was no longer Bizet's *Carmen*. London's grand premiere in 1878 was in Italian. With some skill, Guiraud had composed music for the recitatives, but it weakened the original contrast created by numbers in different keys. Gone was also the effect when after many dialogues Don José sings: "Parle-moi de ma mere." José does not sing the first time he meets Carmen. He doesn't sing until Micaëla speaks of his mother and he yearns to hear more. Adding the gypsy dance from *Jolie fille* and the farandole from *L'Arlésienne* as ballet to act 4 also changed the work considerably. Finally, concessions to performer whims increasingly transformed Bizet's transparent opera comique style into the old style of grand opera.

Thoughtless production practices and a "horrible German version"[5] by Hopp (who went on to mutilate *La Jolie fille de Perth*) shaped *Carmen*'s countenance for German audiences, resulting in numerous misconceptions and distortions of the entire narrative. One standard German compendium still relates the story of Carmen starting with "The good sergeant truly loves . . . the simple peasant girl. . . ."[6] In Germany Escamillo's ambiguous couplet refrain "Toréador en garde," originally intended to be sung *piano/leggiero*, became a martial "off to the battle"[7] favorite in musical request programs.

In 1907 *Carmen* was shown for the first time at Palais Garnier—the Opéra could simply no longer ignore this indisputably most important French opera. At the Opéra Comique the work was produced as it was originally composed, but prominent singers were not engaged and thus the tradition of *Carmen* there remained peripheral. Under the direction of André Cluytens, in 1950 the Opéra did play the Opéra Comique's version for a recording. More than any other version, it provides an authentic musical impression of what Bizet's work was supposed to sound like, even though the lack of voice and instrumental mastery reduces the pleasure. Sir Thomas Beecham's composite recording from 1959 is still the most satisfactory in terms of style and enormous vocal quality, although it is based on the edition with recitatives.

Later, when famous singers and conductors and large recording companies took an interest in the original version of *Carmen*, they neglected to assemble casts that made idiomatic sense. The result was several new recordings with names of great singers with experience in Bayreuth and Verdi operas that nonetheless sang this thoroughly French opera[8] for the most part with considerable American, Greek, Italian, and Spanish accents. Outside of Paris and the Opéra Comique, until the end of the twentieth century *Carmen* was mostly shown in the version with recitatives. Only the German stage soon returned to the original version: in 1933 at the opera in Cologne directed by a National Socialist, and then again in 1949 in Soviet-occupied Berlin, where Walter Felsenstein presented versions that included spoken dialogues, as Clemens Krauss had done prior to the Second World War at the Bavarian State Opera.

In 1964 musicologist Fritz Oeser (1911–1982) published a new edition of *Carmen* that despite all justified objections to editorial details has gradually gained recognition, not only for performances sung in German (using Felsenstein's translation), but also for productions in French. Oeser's edition allows an optional use of the controversial recitatives, which seemed advisable at the time in order to facilitate renunciation of the "traditional" version that had been used on German stages (with a few timid attempts to revise it) since 1875. Oeser's work was pioneering for the reception of *Carmen*, but it does not relieve opera houses of the task of putting thought into how they want to present this opera. A supplement includes suggestions for all kinds of variation, but fifty years later, Oeser's edition is still practical. The supplement revived music for *Carmen* that had not been heard for decades, namely, a passage that Bizet later composed during rehearsals at the wish of a singer. It is a sophisticated solo, but wholly irrelevant to the plot: "Scène et pantomime" with a couplet for Sergeant Moralès from act 1. During Bizet's lifetime it had been dropped from productions and therefore was not included in later scores and piano arrangements. In 1970 Rafael Frühbeck de Burgos included it in his recording of *Carmen* at EMI. Despite dialogues dubbed by actors and an "overqualified" Don José, it remains one of the most authentic recordings.

Posterity must come to terms with the fact that in principle three sources exist for *Carmen* and all of them can be used without remorse: the composer's autograph score that reveals how he originally imagined the opera; material for the original premiere that contains changes made during rehearsals; and finally the first printed piano arrangement, which does not contain all of the modifications.

Of considerable philological interest is therefore Michael Rot's critical edition from 2008 that discusses all of these sources.[9] But unfortunately it unnecessarily tempts producers to use the inauthentic recitatives so convenient for international opera. Richard Langham Smith[10] has also published a new edition of the score for *Carmen* based on a CD recording (sung in English),[11] but one can hardly detect deviations from Oeser's notes. Langham Smith's intent was to provide performance material suitable for historical presentations. In 2009 his score was used for a production at the Opéra Comique,[12] conducted by John Eliot Gardiner. Gardiner kept some of the passages of the score that had been omitted for the CD recording under the direction of David Parry. Although his musicians and singers worked to create the original sound, the outcome does not give us any particularly new insight into the work.

Of greater significance for modern opera houses is Robert Didion's work that includes uncensored dialogue text, allowing an authentic production of *Carmen* as opéra comique without the extensive preparation that Oeser's edition involves. From Didion's version (Schott), ironically only the above-mentioned scene for Moralès was chosen for a CD recording[13] that in 2003 in otherwise postmodern arbitrariness on the one hand returns to Guiraud's recitatives as had been done a century before, but on the other hand presents a hitherto unpublished air for the heroine accompanied by a chorus that using the same text was once meant as a substitute for the havanaise. The number is rather lightweight in a traditional fashion and could have been written by either Thomas or Gounod, which is probably why Bizet dropped it.

A disregard for the wealth of interrelatedness between the music and the text in Bizet's compositions began right at the composer's own funeral. Bizet would have been more forgiving of the fact that they gave him a religious funeral (at the Église de la Trinité on 5 June 1875) than that at the ceremony Bouhy (who sang Escamillo) and Duchesne (tenor) sang the duet from *The Pearl Fishers* to the text of "Pie Jesu." Pasdeloup, to whom Bizet had dedicated the score for *Carmen*, did the conducting. The church organist improvised on, among other things, *Carmen*! The cortege counted four thousand people, but his widow was not among them; she lay ill at Ludovic Halévy's home. Bizet's closest relative at the funeral was his father Adolphe, who was to survive his son by eleven years. Gounod, Thomas, du Locle, and Camille Doucet[14] were

Bizet's grave at Père-Lachaise. *Courtesy of C. Schwandt*

the pallbearers; Bizet was interred at the cemetery Père-Lachaise. That evening the Opéra Comique staged a special performance of *Carmen*. Paul Dubois, a respected sculptor that Bizet had met in Rome, made the bust for Bizet's grave. Marie and Jean Reiter lived with Adolphe Bizet until his death in 1886. Geneviève Bizet, at the age of twenty-six a widow on her sixth wedding anniversary, inherited after her mother's death in 1884 the rights to works by her father, Jacques Fromental Halévy, which all together made less profit than *Carmen*. In 1886 she married lawyer and art lover Émile Straus, who worked for the Rothschild family. Renowned artists were guests at her private salon, including some who took sides with Jewish officer Dreyfus, falsely accused of treason. Jacques Bizet developed a dependency on alcohol and other substances and in 1922 committed suicide, fifteen days before the death of his friend from youth, Marcel Proust, who had been infelicitously in love with him. Geneviève Straus had been Proust's patroness; she died in 1926. It is said that Oriane de Guermantes in Proust's *In Search of Lost Time* resembles her.

Notes

1. Walter Felsenstein, *Schriften zum Musiktheater* (Berlin, 1976), 232.

2. *La Boulangère a des écus*, premiered on 10 October 1875 at the Théâtre des Variétés.

3. *La Tragédie de Carmen*, 1983 (film version Alby Film/Antenne 2).

4. Rémy Stricker, *Georges Bizet* (Paris, 1999), 271.

5. Kurt Honolka, *Kulturgeschichte des Librettos* (Wilhelmshaven, 1979), 115.

6. Rudolf Kloiber and Wulf Konold, *Handbuch der Oper*, 12th ed. (Kassel, 2004).

7. *Auf in den Kampf!*

8. Martin Cooper, *Georges Bizet* (London, 1938), 129. Cooper writes that *Carmen* is "French to the core."

9. Published by Verlagsgruppe Hermann Wien, n.d.

10. Edition Peters, n.d.

11. Chandos, 2003.

12. DVD for the label FRA Musica.

13. Directed by Michel Plasson for EMI.

14. Theater writer, member of the Académie française, and president of the Societé des Auteurs et Compositeurs Dramatiques (SACD) that still exists today.

Selected Bibliography

Bizet's Letters and Records

Briefe aus Rom 1857–1860. Edited and translated into German by Walter Klefisch. Hamburg, 1949.

Correspondence with Charles Gounod. *Revue de Paris*, 15 December 1899.

de Betzi, Gaston [Georges Bizet]. "Causerie musicale." *Revue Nationale et Étrangère*, 3 August 1867.

Letters to Ernest Guiraud, in Mina Curtiss, "Unpublished Letters by Georges Bizet," *Musical Quarterly* 3 (1950).

Letters to Paul Lacombe, in Hugues Imbert, *Portraits et études*. Paris, 1894.

Lettres (1850–1875): Choisies et présentées par Claude Glayman. Paris, 1989.

Lettres à un ami, 1865–1872. Edited by Edmond Galabert. Paris, 1909.

Lettres: Impressions de Rome, 1857–1860. La Commune, 1871. Edited by Louis Ganderax. Paris, 1908.

Notes de voyage, 1861. Manuscript. Bibliothèque Nationale, Paris.

Books

Bellaigue, Camille. *Georges Bizet: Sa Vie et son œuvre.* Paris, 1891.

Bondeville, Emmanuel. *Georges Bizet tel qu'il fut.* Paris, 1975.

Brancour, René. *La Vie et l'œuvre de Georges Bizet.* Paris, 1913.

Bruk, Mira. *Bizet.* Moscow, 1938.

Cardoze, Michel. *Georges Bizet.* Paris, 1982.

Cooper, Martin. *Georges Bizet.* London, 1938.

Corapi, Giogio. *Invito all'ascolta di Georges Bizet.* Milan, 1992.

Curtiss, Mina. *Bizet and His World*. New York, 1958.

Dean, Winton. *Bizet*. London, 1975 (revised reprint of the 1965 edition, which was a reprint of the 1948 edition).

Delmas, Marc. *Georges Bizet*. Paris, 1930.

Galabert, Edmond. *Georges Bizet: Souvenirs et Correspondance*. Paris, 1877.

Gatti, Guido M. *Giorgio Bizet*. Turin, 1914.

Gauthier-Villars, Henri [Émile Vuillermoz]. *Bizet*. Paris, 1911.

Gerver, Frans. *Georges Bizet*. Brussels, 1945.

Grélinger, Charles. *Bizet*. Paris, n.d., ca. 1915.

Imbert, Hugues. *Georges Bizet*. Paris, 1899.

Kremlev, J. U. *Georges Bizet*. Leningrad, 1935.

Lacombe, Hervé. *Georges Bizet: Naissance d'une identité créatrice*. Paris, 2000.

Landormy, Paul. *Bizet*. Paris, 1924.

Lockspeiser, E. *Bizet*. London, 1946.

Malherbe, Henry. *Georges Bizet*. Paris, 1921.

Mastrigli, Leopoldo. *Giorgio Bizet: La sua vita e le sue opère*. Rome, 1888.

Parker, Douglas Charles. *Georges Bizet: His Life and His Works*. London, 1926. Reprint, 1952.

Pigot, Charles. *Georges Bizet et son œuvre*. Paris, 1886.

Rabe, Julius. *Georges Bizet*. Stockholm, 1925.

Ratiu, Ileana. *Bizet*. Bucharest, 1974.

Renaudin, André. *Georges Bizet es ses parents en cinq énigmes*. Rouen, 1975.

Robert, Frédéric. *Georges Bizet*. Paris, 1965.

Roy, Jean. *Bizet*. Paris, 1983.

Stefan, Paul. *Georges Bizet*. Zurich, 1952.

Stricker, Rémy. *Georges Bizet*. Paris, 1999.

Velikovich, E. J. *Georges Bizet*. Leningrad, 1969.

Voss, Paul. *Georges Bizet*. Leipzig, 1899.

Vuillermoz, Émile. *See* Gauthier-Villars, Henri.

Weissmann, Adolf. *Bizet*. Berlin, 1907.

Wright, Leslie Allison. *Bizet before Carmen*. Ann Arbor, Mich., 1983.

Periodicals

Musica. Special number 6 (1912).

Revue de Musicologie. Special number 11 (1938).

Title Index

Note: Currently the most reliable list of Bizet's complete works can be found in the encyclopedia Die Musik in Geschichte und Gegenwart (vol. 2, columns 1712–1717), second edition, edited by Ludwig Finscher, Cassel 1999. Winton Dean's list of Bizet's works published in 1948 (with its idiosyncratic "WD" numbering that counts a total of 136 works) is untenable. It names as operas ten titles that the composer had only vaguely pondered as potential projects.

* Either merely intended, left unfinished, or lost

Absence 75
Adieu à Suzon 74
Arlésienne Suite 2, 111

Carmen 1–4, 38, 50n6, 60, 64, 65, 72, 74, 79, 80, 83, 102, 104, 110–112, 114, 116, 117–133
*Carmen saeculare, a cantata 34
Chanson d'avril 75
Chasse fantastique 70
Clovis et Clotilde, a cantata 28–30

*David, a cantata 24
Djamileh 74, 99–105, 110
Don Procopio 37, 38, 42, 43, 53, 56, 80, 81

Funeral March in B minor 92

Grande valse de concert in E flat major 16
*Grisélidis 94, 99, 110, 115, 123
Guitare 74

Ivan IV 62–67, 80, 92, 100, 103, 126, 127

Jeux d'enfants for four hands at the piano 99–101

La Chanson du fou 75
*La Chasse d'Ossian 53, 70
*La Coupe du roi de Thulé 91, 113

La Jolie fille de Perth 3, 67n2, 77, 78, 80, 81, 84, 89, 111, 129
La Maison du docteur 21–22
La Rose et l'abeille 16
L'Âme triste est pareille au doux ciel 17n4, 74
L'Arlésienne 2, 50n6, 108–111, 118, 126, 129
Le Docteur miracle 25, 31, 56
Les Adieux de l'hôtesse arabe 74, 103
Les Pêcheurs de perles 3, 59–62, 126, 132

Marlborough s'en va-t-en guerre 87

Nocturne No. 1 in F major 16

Overture in A minor 19

Pastorale 74
Patrie! . . . 114–116
Petite Marguerite 16
Petite suite 100–101, 126

Quatre préludes (C major, A minor, G major, and E minor) 15

Roma, a symphony in C major 45–50, 53, 92, 104
Romance sans paroles 16

Saint-Jean de Patmos, for four male voices 81
Scherzo (reused in *Roma*) and Funeral March in F minor 48, 53, 54
Six chants du Rhin 70–76
Sonnet 74
Symphony in C Major 3, 19–20, 26n3, 38

Te Deum, for soloists, choir, and orchestra 33–34
Théme brilliant in C major 15
Three pieces published in the *Magasin des familles* 16
Trois Esquisses 40

Variations chromatiques 90, 100
Vasco da Gama, a symphonic ode 45–50, 55, 64, 92, 103

Waltz in C major 15

Name Index

Adam, Adolphe, 12, 77, 87
Adenis, Jules, 77, 80
Adler, Guido, 3
Almeida, Antonio, 19
Auber, Daniel-François-Esprit, 8, 12, 14, 16, 25, 41, 43, 45, 47, 57, 77, 79, 88, 99, 118

Bach, Johann Sebastian, 12, 15, 69
Balanchine, George, 21
Banville, Théodore de, 128
Barbier, Jules, 25, 52, 53, 77, 84
Barthe, Adrien, 65
Battu, Léon, 34
Beecham, Sir Thomas, 130
Beethoven, Ludwig van, 2, 8, 12, 19, 20, 21, 41, 42, 54, 70, 76, 79
Bellini, Vincenzo, 8, 12, 15, 31, 59, 69
Bénazet, Édouard, 55
Berlioz, Hector, 9, 12, 19, 22, 28, 29, 33, 34, 45, 46, 47, 49, 55, 61, 62, 63, 74, 75, 78, 92, 101, 116
Bischoffsheim, Raphael, 88
Bismarck, Otto von, 95, 76

Bizet, Adolphe, 5, 8, 12, 72, 107, 133
Bizet, Aimée, 5, 7, 52
Bizet, Geneviève, 17, 63, 86, 87, 92, 94, 97, 107, 121, 129, 133
Bizet, Jacques, 107, 122, 133
Blau, Édouard, 91, 113
Boccaccio, Giovanni, 94
Boieldieu, Adrien, 8, 12, 14, 78
Bonaparte, Napoleon, 19, 57
Bonaparte, Princess Mathilde-Létizia Wilhelmine, 73
Boucher, Maurice le, 72
Bouffar, Zulma, 120
Bouhy, 132
Bouilhet, Louis, 75
Brook, Peter, 2, 127
Bülow, Hans von, 51
Burion, Amédée, 28
Busnach, William, 88, 97, 188
Busser, Henri, 88

Cambiaggio, Carlo, 37
Carafa, Michèle Enrico, 31, 34, 45
Cardoze, Michel, 57, 72, 73

Carré, Michel, 25, 52, 53, 57, 59, 77, 84
Carvalho, Léon (Léon Carvaille), 56–57, 61–62, 65, 76–78, 80–82, 88, 107, 109
Castro y Bellvís, Guillén de, 114
Chantavoine, Jean, 21, 65
Charpentier, Marc-Antoine, 24, 33
Chéri, Victor, 28, 62
Cherubini, Luigi, 8, 10, 12, 14
Chopin, Frédéric, 12, 15, 50, 90
Choudens, Antoine de, 16, 61, 66, 69, 76, 84, 85, 92, 115, 124
Cimarosa, Domenico, 33, 37
Clairin, Georges, 84, 102, 124
Clappison, Antoine-Louis, 45–46, 50, 77, 88
Clotilde, Queen, 30
Clovis, King, 30
Cluytens, André, 130
Colbert, Jean-Baptiste, 22
Colin, Charles, 31
Colonna-Walewski, Alexandre Comte de, 56
Colonne, Édouard, 100, 111
Columbus, Christopher, 46
Constant, Marius, 127
Cooper, Martin, 100
Cormon, Eugène, 57, 59, 118
Corneille, Pierre, 114
Courbet, Gustave, 97
Curtiss, Mina, 33, 48, 66, 116

Dalayrac, Nicolas, 57
Daudet, Alphonse, 96–97, 107–111
Dautresme, Auguste-Lucien, 87
David, Félicien, 24, 45, 46, 55, 57, 59, 74, 76
Dean, Winton, 17, 34, 39, 57, 65, 72, 74, 92, 99, 109, 116
Debussy, Claude, 15
Deffès, Louis Pierre, 139
Delaborde, Élie Miriam, 129
Delacroix, Eugène, 17

Delâtre, Louis, 47
Delibes, Léo, 87
Delsarte, Aimée. See Bizet, Aimée
Delsarte, François Alexandre, 6, 8, 76
Delsarte, Jean-Nicolas, 5
Delsarte, Rosine, 8
Devin-Duvivier, Adolphe, 82
Devriès, Jane, 80
Díaz de la Peña, Eugenio, 91
Díaz de Vivar, Don Rodrigo, 114
Didion, Robert, 131
D'Ivry, Paul, 22
Donizetti, Gaetano, 8, 12, 15, 25, 31, 37, 38, 78, 82
Douay, Georges, 97
Doucet, Camille, 132
Dubois, François Clément Théodore, 57
Dubois, Paul, 133
Duchesne, M., 132
Dukas, Paul, 15
Dumas, Alexandre, 27
Durand (publisher), 100
Duvevrier, Charles, 16

Elssler, Fanny, 13
Érard, Pierre, 51
Escudier, Léon, 150
Eugénie, Empress of France, 52, 70, 72, 94, 108

Faure, Jean-Baptiste, 112–114
Felsenstein, Walter, 118, 130
Fioravanti, Vincenzo, 37
Fischer-Dieskau, Dietrich, 75
Flaubert, Gustave, 24, 57
Flotow, Friedrich von, 12, 77
Franz Joseph, Emperor of Austria, 40
Frühbeck de Burgos, Rafael, 131

Galabert, Edmond, 65, 79, 86, 91, 92, 111
Gallet, Louis, 91, 99, 104, 113–114
Galli-Marié, Célestine, 104, 120

Gama, Vasco da, 46, 47
Gardiner, John Eliot, 111, 131
Gauthier-Villars, Henri, 65, 136
Gautier, Théophile, 16, 74, 75
Gebsattel, Jérôme, 78
Gerigk, Herbert, 21
Gevaert, François Auguste, 53
Giacomotti, Félix-Henri, 32, 39
Gilbert, Alphonse, 9
Girard, William, 22
Glayman, Claude, 89
Gluck, Christoph Willibald Ritter von, 6, 70
Godard, Benjamin, 61
Goethe, Johann Wolfgang von, 52, 77, 78, 91
Gossec, François-Joseph, 33
Gould, Glenn, 91
Gounod, Charles, 1, 5, 10, 12, 13, 16, 19, 20, 22, 25, 29, 31, 32, 40, 45, 47, 48, 53, 55, 60, 62–64, 66, 69, 73, 77–79, 84, 91, 92, 94, 104, 109, 112, 121, 131, 132
Gruyer (Guardi), Hector, 5, 40
Guiraud, Ernest, 8, 15, 48, 66, 91, 101, 111, 114, 121, 127, 129, 131
Guiraud, Jean-Baptiste, 8, 9

Halanzier-Dufresnoy, Olivier, 113–114
Halévy, Esther, 17, 63, 87
Halévy, Geneviève. See Geneviève Bizet
Halévy, Hannah Léonie, 17, 34, 53, 87, 92, 94, 97, 122
Halévy, Jacques François Fromental Élie, 12, 13, 14, 15, 17, 19, 22, 25, 51, 53, 62, 63, 93, 133
Halévy, Léon, 17, 87, 88
Halévy, Ludovic, 25, 82–83, 94, 108, 111, 112, 118, 127, 129, 132
Hammerstein, Oscar, 2
Hammond, Arthur, 61
Handel, George Frideric, 12, 110
Hanslick, Eduard, 3, 49, 83, 100, 104

Hartmann (publisher), 69
Hartmann, Ernst, 65
Haussmann, Georges-Eugène, 11, 124
Haydn, Joseph, 19, 54
Heim, Joseph-Eugène, 31–32
Heine, Heinrich, 15
Heller, Stephen, 90
Hérold, Louis Joseph Ferdinand, 12, 118
Hervé, Florimond, 12
Heugel (publisher), 69, 70, 74, 89
Hoffmann, Ernst Theodor Amadeus, 25, 28, 38, 87
Homer, 45–46
Hopp, Julius, 3, 79, 129
Horace, 34
Hugo, Victor, 38, 70, 74, 75, 81, 97

Ingres, Jean-Auguste-Dominique, 32
Ivan the Terrible, 55

Jauner, Franz von, 129
Jérôme Bonaparte, King of Westphalia, 73
Joncières, Victorin de, 82, 128
Jones, David Lloyd, 78

Kalbeck, Max, 78, 79
Karamsin, Nikolai M., 63
Klefisch, Walter, 2
Kracauer, Siegfried, 83
Krauss, Clemens, 130
Kreutzer, Conradin, 55

Lacombe, Hervé, 66
Lacombe, Paul, 84, 91
Lamartine, Alphonse de, 17, 26, 74
Langham Smith, Richard, 131
Lecocq, Alexandre Charles, 25, 104
Legouix, Isidore-Édouard, 88
Leonardo da Vinci, 32
Leoncavallo, Ruggero, 1, 110
Leopold, Prince of Hohenzollern-Sigmaringen, 95

L'Épine, Ernest, 107
Leroy, François-Hippolyte, 62
Lesseps, Ferdinand de, 94
Leuven, Adolphe de, 99, 111, 118, 120
Levy, Henri, 57
Liszt, Franz, 51, 57, 71
Locle, Camille du, 83, 94, 99, 111, 118, 120, 121, 124, 127, 128, 129, 132
Lortzing, Albert, 12
Louis XIV of France, 11, 22, 87
Louis-Napoléon. See Napoleon III
Lubitsch, Ernst, 2
Lucas, Hippolyte, 57
Ludwig II, King of Bavaria, 97
Lully, Jean-Baptiste, 6

Mac-Mahon, Patrice de, 99, 124
Macpherson, James, 52
Maglanowich, Hyacinthe, 52
Magnard, Albéric, 101
Mahler, Gustav, 49, 104
Malherbe, Charles, 43
Manet, Édouard, 97
Maria Stuart, 94
Marlborough, John Churchill, Duke of, 87–88
Marmontel, Antoine François, 8–9, 12, 50, 70
Marschner, Heinrich, 12, 79
Massenet, Jules, 91, 101, 104–105, 114, 116
Massy, M., 84
Mathilde Bonaparte, Princess, 73
Maximilian I, Emperor of Mexico, 59
Méhul, Étienne Nicolas, 12
Meifred, Joseph Émile, 8
Meihac, Henri, 82, 83, 111, 112, 118, 127
Mendelssohn Bartholdy, Felix, 48–49, 53, 54, 101
Mercadante, Saverio, 37
Mérimée, Prosper, 2, 52, 95, 111, 117–118, 121

Méry, Joseph, 70, 73, 83
Meyerbeer, Giacomo, 2, 12, 14, 15, 18, 42, 47, 63, 64, 79, 82
Michelangelo Buonarroti, 42
Miolan, Caroline, 76
Mistral, Frédéric, 31, 94
Mogador, Céleste, 72–73
Molière, 38, 40
Moltke, Helmuth von, 76
Montréal, Mlle. de, 24
Moore, Thomas, 57
Moreton de Chabrillan, Lionel Comte de, 72
Morny, Charles, Duc de, 107, 118
Mosca, Giuseppe, 37
Mozart, Wolfgang Amadeus, 2, 8, 12, 19, 21, 33, 34, 40–42, 54, 57, 61, 69, 70, 76, 95, 127
Musset, Alfred de, 72, 74, 99, 100, 113
Musset, Paul de, 100

Napoleon I, Emperor of France, 11, 56, 73, 97
Napoleon III, Emperor of France, 11, 32, 40, 56, 76, 82, 94, 95, 108, 112, 124
Negri, Pola, 2
Nicolai, Otto, 77
Nietzsche, Friedrich, 3
Nilsson, Christine, 69, 80, 84, 89

Oeser, Fritz, 130
Offenbach, Jacques, 11, 12, 15, 24–27, 38, 60, 72, 79, 82, 83, 95, 100, 111, 118, 120
Orsini, Felice, 40

Pacini, Antonio, 77
Pacini, Giovanni, 37
Paer, Ferdinando, 33
Paladilhe, Émile, 104
Parker, Douglas Charles, 21
Parry, David, 131

Pasdeloup, Jules Étienne, 54, 92, 110, 111, 114, 131
Patti, Adelina, 69, 72
Pergolesi, Giovanni Battista, 120
Perrin, Émile, 83, 91
Piestre, Pierre-Étienne, 57
Pigot, Charles, 3, 57, 127
Pius IX, Pope, 40
Planté, Francis, 50
Planté, Gaston, 49–50
Plasson, Michel, 101, 111, 133
Ponsard, François, 45
Preminger, Otto, 2
Prokofiev, Sergei, 21
Proust, Marcel, 133
Puccini, Giacomo, 2, 94, 110

Racine, Jean, 114
Rameau, Jean-Philippe, 6, 24
Raphael, 42
Ravel, Maurice, 101
Reber, Napoléon Henri, 45
Regnault, Henri, 84
Reiter, Jean, 52, 87, 122, 133
Reiter, Marie, 51, 52, 63, 107, 129, 133
Reyer, Ernest, 47, 55, 70, 101, 124, 128
Richardson, Samuel, 94
Rizzio, David, 94
Rodrigues, Hippolyte, 94
Rodrigues-Henriques, Édouard, 34
Romani, Felice, 31, 37
Ronsard, Pierre de, 74, 76
Rossignol, Félix-Ludger, 82
Rossini, Gioachino, 12, 15, 25, 27, 30–34, 37, 38, 41, 47, 48, 77, 80, 113
Rot, Michael, 131
Rothschild (family), 133
Roze, Marie, 119

Saint-Georges, Jules-Henri Vernoy de, 77, 80, 82
Saint-Saëns, Camille, 47, 50, 71, 84, 103, 104

Sardou, Victorien, 94, 114
Satie, Erik, 15
Saura, Carlos, 2
Sax, Adolphe, 109
Schiller, Friedrich, 83
Schnetz, Jean-Victor, 32, 39
Schubert, Franz, 75, 79, 101
Schumann, Robert, 50, 57, 72, 100–101
Scott, Sir Walter, 77–82, 88
Scribe, Eugène, 16, 25, 37, 41, 51, 63, 77, 78, 87, 88
Sellier, Charles, 31, 32
Shakespeare, William, 38, 55, 78
Shchedrin, Rodion, 2
Smetana, Bedřich, 1
Spontini, Gaspare, 12, 59
Staël, Anne Louise Germaine Baronne de, 70
Stefan Grünfeld, Paul, 3
Straus, Émile, 133
Straus, Geneviève. See Bizet, Geneviève
Strauss, Johann, 83, 111
Strauss, Richard, 119
Sue, Eugène, 82
Syagrius, 30

Tassart, Maurice, 65
Tchaikovsky, Peter I., 1, 48
Thomas, Ambroise, 13, 25, 43, 69, 77, 89, 99
Thomson, Bryden, 66
Tizian, 32
Trélat, Marie Molinos, 91, 105
Trianon, Henri, 62–63
Turgenev, Ivan, 121

Vaz de Camões, Luís, 46
Verdi, Giuseppe, 2, 12, 15, 16, 27, 29, 31, 32, 37, 38, 41, 42, 64, 70, 74, 76, 79, 83, 94, 113, 125
Vergil, 46
Vernet, Horace, 32
Véron, Louis-Désiré, 13

Viardot, Pauline, 72, 101, 121
Vittorio Emanuele II, King of Italy, 41
Voss, Egon, 21, 101
Vuillermoz, Émile. *See* Gauthier-Villars, Henri

Wagner, Richard, 2, 3, 4n8, 12, 14, 38, 41, 47, 48, 51, 64, 74, 75, 76, 79, 92, 97, 101, 102, 103, 121, 125
Weber, Carl Maria von, 12, 25, 33, 47, 48, 54, 70, 79, 92

Weingartner, Felix von, 21, 91
Weissmann, Adolf, 3
Wilhelm I, German Emperor, 95
Wolf, Hugo, 80
Wolff, Hellmuth Christian, 102

Yradier, Sebastián de, 72, 123

Zimmermann, Pierre Joseph Guillaume, 10, 13, 14
Zola, Émile, 97